P9-DTL-153

SMALL FIRES

SMALL FIRES

-

AN EPIC IN
THE KITCHEN

REBECCA MAY JOHNSON

CARLSBAD CITY LIBRARY
DISCARD
CARLSBAD CA 92011

Pushkin Press
Somerset House, Strand, London WC2R 1LA

The right of Rebecca May Johnson to be identified as the
author of this Work has been asserted by her in accordance
with the Copyright, Designs & Patents Act 1988

Copyright © 2022 Rebecca May Johnson

Small Fires was first published by Pushkin Press in 2022

5 7 9 8 6 4

ISBN 13: 978-1-91159-048-4

All rights reserved. No part of this publication may be reproduced,
stored in a retrieval system or transmitted in any form or by
any means, electronic, mechanical, photocopying, recording or
otherwise, without prior permission in writing from Pushkin Press

Ruth Rogers recipe from 'Top foodies choose their favourite
recipes of all time' © Guardian News & Media Ltd 2021

Extract from *The Essentials of Italian Cooking* by
Marcella Hazen © Pan Macmillan 2012. Reproduced
with permission of the Licensor through PLSclear

Epigraph from 'Untitled' from *Who Is Mary Sue?*
© Sophie Collins, published by Faber and Faber Ltd, 2018

Designed and typeset by Tetragon, London
Printed and bound by Clays Ltd, Elcograf S.p.A.

www.pushkinpress.com

SEP 2 0 2023

for Zoë

Contents

The village is always on fire.
Men stay away from the kitchens,
take up in outhouses with concrete floors,
while the women – soot in their hair –
initiate the flames into their small routines.

'Untitled', Sophie Collins

Poor fool! His food and drink are not of earth.

'Prologue in Heaven', *Faust*,
Goethe, trans. Anna Swanwick

Prologue in the Kitchen

I tried to write about cooking, but I wrote a hot red epic.

Not sea spray on my skin, but sauce spattering from a pan. The heat of small fires. Tying and untying my apron strings. A recipe that is both the ship that carries me and the hot red sea. In this book, I tell the complicated story of cooking for ten or more years in ten or more kitchens. I tell of the people I encounter, whose desires and refusals rewrite the recipe a thousand times. I tell of what I have learnt.

The contents of this book might have vanished unrecorded – cooked and eaten and washed up, leaving no trace. Documenting what I do in the kitchen can feel like the task of recording almost nothing. But it is the nothing that I am doing, and do almost every day, and have been doing every day for over a decade. It is the nothing that has been part of almost every social interaction of my life as an adult and through which I have come to know almost all the people I love. It is the nothing through which I have been sustained and transformed.

Ten years or more learning to think and to cook unfold in separate spaces, officially at least. I am taught that the work of critical thinking takes place outside of the kitchen, and that cooking in domestic space is not connected to the endeavour of serious thought. It is an exclusion that has limited the shape of our ideas: an imaginative drought, a half-light. If food and thinking coincide, it is in an image of men who have been served dinner, talking face-to-face over the table.

Slowly I realize that when I cook, I am also researching the relationship between the body and language, between self and other; I am learning how to think against a rationalist and patriarchal history of knowledge. This book is a document of that realization: a text that allows cooking into the frame of critical enquiry and in which critical enquiry is shaped by cooking. This does not mean exchanging the kitchen for the library; my clothes must become spattered with oil.

In this book I think about how I wear an apron, use a knife and apply heat with the same attention I apply to the world outside the kitchen. I think about cooking without glossing over its complexity such as I have experienced it. This is an epic of desire, of dancing, of experiments in embodiment and transformative encounters with other people. I want to blow up the kitchen and rebuild it to cook again, critically alert, seeking pleasure and revelation.

Recipe for beginning an epic:

Begin the epic by summoning a body. It will take some effort, so a pumpkin or similar may help. Then decide how to clothe yourself for what lies ahead, and how to dismantle the traps you will encounter on your journey.

Apron Strings

I begin on the sofa unable to find a reason to get up; I am rescued by a pumpkin and by apron strings.

AUGUST 2018

9.15 a.m.
On the sofa and I can't get up. I call you to tell you that I cannot write, and you tell me how I've got up off the sofa before and spoon my sentences back to me, reheated. And there's the pumpkin over there, curing on the sunny windowsill. The grazes on its skin from the rough paving outside have hardened and scarred over, a protective dressing: *auto-amour.*

9.27 a.m.
In the kitchen I look at my knives. I take the heaviest in my hand and let its weight drop onto the green exterior of the pumpkin that I've placed on the wooden chopping

board. It is very hard, difficult to cut. I grip the handle firmly and push down, flexing my biceps. The blade slices through the flesh suddenly, shockingly. Each piece rocks back on the board, bright orange.

7.18 p.m.
I put on an apron and stand one leg on the grey-veneer IKEA coffee table. The table is in front of a large mirror that hangs behind the sofa and I look at myself. I feel like I am planting a flag on a mountain, *big dick energy*; I take a photograph. Underneath the apron, which I am wearing tied tight and close to my body so it resists my expanding chest as I breathe, are baggy trousers and a men's short-sleeved shirt. After looking at the photo on the phone screen I return to the kitchen and melt a sliver of blue cheese into double cream and check on the pumpkin.

7.59 p.m.
Back on the sofa. Soft now, the orange pumpkin slices fan out on the white plate. Blue cream partly covers them like sheets sliding off a bed.

*

Do you have positive feelings about aprons?

Yes and no.

Strings!

The erotics of tying my apron strings, tightly. I prefer aprons made from pliable cotton cloth. After experimentation I find I need fabric soft enough to wrap round my body and then bind it, an embrace for which stiffer fabrics won't do. I fold up a little of the lower half of the apron to make a corset and pull the strings taut, cinching in. As I cook, the dig of strings into my skin reminds me to keep thinking with my body. Strings under tension bring me back here again here again here again, now again, now.

Long ago, tying an apron felt like tying myself up (and not in a way I would have chosen). Aprons are still threaded through with the image of 'natural' feminine destiny, the kind that makes me uncomfortable, that makes me feel like running away.

Cut your apron strings!

I find pleasure in the movement between masculine and feminine. A perpetual undoing. Clothes underneath constrained by the apron ties on top. I need to occupy more than one position at the same time, to construct a superposition of both and neither and then something else too, an opening elsewhere. I find myself in the unresolved movement between different gendered styles. An outfit that is always undoing itself is the best one for me and for my enquiries in the kitchen.

My apron strings return me to my body in the ways I want them to – a binding I have chosen to play with – they maintain the possibility of both, *and, and...*

here I am!

I've been here in the kitchen for ten years or more –

> tying and untying the strings
> wearing an apron and making it disappear
> *at the same time*,
> trying to weave a different kind of apron

The illusion of essentialized gender shatters for me before I am familiar with the language that dismantles the concept; I feel it. The impulse to break up a sentence in which I cannot see myself and which cannot accommodate the ways I want to move my shoulders. Then philosopher Judith Butler gives me the words to describe my untying, of gender as 'an identity instituted through *a stylized repetition of acts...* bodily gestures, movements, and enactments of various kinds'. (Judith Butler) And it feels even better and my joy intensifies and I dance dance dance in the kitchen reciting these words.

Gender is an embodied style, *for me at least*. Again and again, I untie the strings, and retie them, differently. It takes some practice, some years, but I develop a method for tying that is also an untying, for wearing my apron so that I am not dressing for my own erasure –

THE VOICE OF THE APRON IS *OURS*,

(after Patricia Klindienst Joplin)

> sweats and works and thinks and wants,
>
> has a body

apron is an apron is an apron is an apron

(after Gertrude Stein)

When I cut through the pumpkin my body comes alive. Muscles flex my knife in my hand I feel macho, displaying machismo like the arm-wrestling sailors in Jean Paul Gaultier perfume adverts. I think about the gleaming camp of oil-slicked biceps, their tight t-shirts straining over their muscles and the tight apron strings straining over my chest, the cut halves of pumpkin on the wooden board a sign I have won this match. The pleasure and the difficulty of this physicality, of this work.

What I am doing in this apron is not what you think I am doing
    in this apron.
I have been trying to say something about Being
in the kitchen,
    it isn't easy:

Over ten years or more I return to the apron, to the pan, to the kitchen, again and again in many different kitchens, but it is not repetition, it is insistence. (Gertrude Stein)

Holding a critical position and tasting the sauce, now that's quantum physics!

The Semiotics of the Kitchen

In the kitchen

In the rough waters between Scylla and Charybdis
between a rock and a hard place

between holding a critical position and tasting the sauce,
                              there are a lot of questions.

In the kitchen I am standing in between Martha Rosler
and Nigella Lawson. Criticism and pleasure enter together,
holding hands.

On one side, Martha Rosler –

The artist Martha Rosler makes the argument that a woman
might simply become an extension of a whisk, and demonstrates this in the film *Semiotics of the Kitchen*.

On the other side, Nigella Lawson –

The writer and TV-food-celebrity/icon Nigella Lawson makes the argument that women (and everyone else) should pleasure themselves with what they can produce with a whisk and demonstrates this on television.

*

I tell someone that I am thinking about the kitchen, and she tells me about the artist Martha Rosler and her video, *Semiotics of the Kitchen*. I find it on YouTube and watch: the video begins with a shot of Martha Rosler holding up a sign on a chalkboard that says 'Semiotics of the Kitchen'. Then, slowly, the camera zooms out to show her standing in front of a refrigerator and an oven. It's a modern, electrified kitchen. It is 1975. Rosler puts down the sign and I see that she's wearing a black polo neck. Her hair is worn loose. She picks up an apron and puts it over her clothes. She takes her time fastening it with a button behind her neck and then with a string around her waist and then she says:

'Apron'

Rosler does not make any gestures of welcome, which I find interesting and unusual. Her voice is firm, and it is negative. There is no charm, no musicality in her tone. She is not welcoming me, and she is not hosting me in this kitchen. 'Bowl' comes next, and she picks up a metal mixing bowl and mimes a stirring action. Rosler works her way through the alphabet in this way, picking up an object, making a gesture, saying its name. Her semiotics of the kitchen begins with putting on an apron: dressing appropriately. It is a garment to wear when using kitchen implements, which give specified movements to the apron-wearer. The implements Rosler picks up make shapes out of her body: they *implement her* to their purpose in the kitchen. She becomes secondary, the engine that drives the tools. A is first in the alphabet, and also A is for Apron, an article of clothing to be worn in the kitchen at the beginning of a day's work.

'They say it is love' (Silvia Federici)

In *Wages Against Housework*, published in 1975, the feminist Marxist theorist Silvia Federici argues that house-work is not seen as work because it is considered an expression of love. Federici articulates beautifully how domestic work like cooking is a double bind of work that cannot be consented to or refused *as work*, because of its status as non-work.

When I read this I feel wild,
                              that, through its definition as a gendered expression of love, cooking (among other forms of domestic labour performed both inside and outside the home) is often not properly viewed as work, as labour. I think of how people, and women in particular, are often encouraged to prepare food joyfully and 'instinctively', without breaking sweat or showing signs of fatigue or complaint.

The status of cooking as 'non-work' makes it difficult for those doing it to be seen as workers who might refuse to cook at all, who might do it without a reassuring performance of joy, who might gather and strike, or demand an end to zero-hours contracts and low pay, or demand a universal basic income that recognizes the labour of social reproduction... Who might also disentangle cooking from their very Being so that they can occupy a critical, or enquiring position towards it. Who might at some point cook for their own reasons, or for love of their own body – rather than exclusively to serve the appetites of others, or for someone else's accumulation of capital to the detriment of their own lives.

The continued status of domestic work as barely-work or unskilled work is reflected in the fact that cooking and cleaning and caring are among the most poorly paid and precarious forms of labour in capitalist societies. Low-paid and unpaid domestic work makes it possible to keep wages down in other jobs.

To successfully exploit gendered labour, try using love!

After reading Federici, I realize that what shocks me about Martha Rosler's video is that she drains the kitchen scenario of love, or rather, the performance of love as part of her labour. By refusing to perform 'happiness', Rosler shows the viewer that this is ordinarily also part of the job. 'More smiles? More money.' (Federici) Smiling is the work that conceals the work: without it, we realize that it is *all*

22

work. The movements of Rosler's body in *Semiotics of the Kitchen* are jerky and mechanical, as if she is an automaton. There is none of the gladness of 1970s American cookery shows. The happy housewife has become a knife, a fork, a juicer, a tenderizer...

'We are shelves, we are / Tables' (Sylvia Plath)

Her body speaks with the grammar of a food-making assembly-line except that, eerily, there is no food. Rosler's knife doesn't slice a carrot, she makes a stabbing motion like the shadow in the shower scene of Alfred Hitchcock's *Psycho*. The blunting effect of domestication is reversed in that moment, and I am reminded that kitchen utensils contain within them the potential to become weapons. Rosler's performance becomes a demonstration of how to use them. Kitchen workers are always-already-fully-armed with knives and fire and the skills to poison...

'So many of us!' (Plath)

Rosler isn't making dinner, she's summoning viewers to smash patriarchy and capitalism with a wooden meat tenderizer!

At the end of the alphabet Rosler uses her knife to slash the letter Z through the air like Zorro the masked liberator. Then she folds her arms and stands still. She has completed the *Semiotics of the Kitchen*. But there is something more, something after Z. Rosler's knife cut the fabric of the kitchen, letting in some light: she shrugs.

Rosler's shrug comes from elsewhere, from beyond the frame of the semiotics of the kitchen. It's not the gesture of a woman whose movements are determined by kitchen implements. Rosler's shrug might be the de-alienation of her body, a display of her self-expression, disinterest, ambivalence. The shrug does not display a love of service; it is a useless, almost playful movement. It is unproductive and a refusal of *progress-towards-dinner*. In another light, Rosler's shrug is as useful as a stick of dynamite. The possibility of something more than unconsented-to work cloaked in the performance of love.

Labours of love that cannot be refused will eventually taste of pain and fury (even if they are exquisite and delicious).

The secret ingredient is solidarity!

✳

In her memoir *The Gastronomical Me*, published in 1943, American food writer M.F.K. Fisher describes Ora, the woman employed to cook for her family. Ora makes food 'exciting and new and delightful' for Fisher and her sister when they are children. Fisher exclaims, 'There are little stars, all made of pie crust! They have seeds on them! Oh, how beautiful! How good!' Ora is even frugal and her exceptional food costs no more than that made by blander cooks. However, the dreamy, poetic voice of Ora's cooking – her pie crust looks up at the stars – is a transgression of her class position in the eyes of Fisher's grandmother, who takes pleasure in expressing her hatred freely. In response to her children's delight, Fisher's mother repeats learned cruelty and tells them not to speak of Ora's food, 'especially when the cook could hear them'. Fisher's mother and grandmother try to keep Ora from knowing her own power, which so explicitly undermines the class hierarchy that divides them. Loyalty to their own class trumps a sense of solidarity with other women. They try to silence the children's uninhibited enthusiasm for Ora's cooking.

But Fisher covertly observes Ora's exquisite knife skills which transform meat, vegetables and herbs into forms that change their flavour. Ora does everything with her beloved knife, 'as if it were part of her hand'. She is in command of her knife (if little else). Fisher's Grandmother recognizes its power; she says it is a 'wicked affectation to have a "French" knife and take it everywhere as if it were alive, and spend all the spare time polishing and sharpening it'. Ora commits suicide with her perfectly sharp French knife.

Oppression sours the milk!
Open a tin of tuna and make yourself a sandwich. Maybe the cook would rather be running down a hill, or driving very fast, or lying very still.

Who cares if a cook makes the most delicious food if the conditions in which they work are exploitative? Who does that serve?

*

Contestants on TV chef competitions often cite dishes cooked by their mother or grandmother as inspiration. They are encouraged to do so by producers in themed episodes. The food cooked by these women is often described as being 'made with love', though this adulation is often accompanied by a comment about its simplicity. The cooks, their emotions and the food are reduced to caricature – there is an image of loving hands preparing the dish, of emotion flowing through the body into a mixing bowl or frying pan. In this narrative, which seems to blight every reference to mother/grandmother cooking in popular British culture, the cook is pure of heart and uncomplaining. Such dream images are deployed by advertisements for gravy granules, pre-made sauces and frozen roast potatoes in which the cook producing the food radiates uncomplicated love. The phrase 'cooking with love' is used to avoid thinking about the cook and the specificity of her life.

What is a cook's life?

When the cook works in conditions so bad that they must go on strike, then people are discouraged from thinking about how a cook's feelings are translated into food. Or if a cook in a domestic setting is cooking when they really do not want to but feel they have no choice, then her emotions are not considered a desirable seasoning. Then there is the fallacy of a cook without a history, without feeling, or body, or voice.

Unromancing and complicating the kitchen is clarifying and helpful. I am grateful to Martha Rosler, to Silvia Federici, to Ora the cook.

*

But I do not have answers to all of my questions. For example, there is no food in *Semiotics of the Kitchen*. Perhaps this absence is necessary. Rosler refuses viewers the visual pleasure of food and the image of the happy housewife in the kitchen and this is what allows us to see work in the kitchen as work. As Sara Ahmed notes, 'Happiness can work to cover over unhappiness, in part by covering over its causes.' The figure of the loving cook feeding us gladly is part of what Rosler and Federici dismantle. No single cook, theorist, writer, or artwork can answer every question in the kitchen, there is always room for another –

Now...

I am hungry!

Nigella smiles to the camera in a pristine kitchen. She wears a pink, twinset-style button-up cardigan. She strokes and pats gleaming implements with the tips of her fingers. She walks downstairs in a satin dressing gown and spoons dessert into her mouth in a dimly lit kitchen. When I am young, I think that Nigella on TV binds the act of cooking to a nostalgic image of the 'Woman in the Kitchen'.

Get the hell out of the kitchen!

('Get the hell out of the kitchen' is what Harriet Lerner, the prominent American clinical psychologist, feminist psychoanalytic theorist and writer said she thought women needed to do to become liberated from men – before she realized that structural oppression was the real problem when she encountered it.)

In the early 2000s when I am at school there is *Ally McBeal* and *Sex and the City* and *Buffy the Vampire Slayer* on the TV. The message in popular culture is that domestic tasks are antithetical to women's liberation. It is a time of 'aspiration' and New Labour Blairite politics. I attend a large local comprehensive school in a rural area and grow up in a white middle-class family. Cookery class at school is called 'Food Technology' and we do more paperwork than cooking. In the prevailing discourse of success and failure, failure to leave the kitchen is framed as failure for women.

Make everything professional!

Our school gets some shiny new buildings funded by government schemes. Up, up, and away! The message is: go to university, get a 'high-powered' office job in a city and be a success. It is a weird political moment where everyone is supposed to 'strive' and become a lawyer or an entrepreneur and then somehow poverty will no longer exist.

The literature we study at my high school is full of white bourgeois women in domestic nightmares, their lives shaped by theories about their mental fragility or 'natural' suitability to forms of labour that exclude them from intellectual life. So, when I see the cover of Nigella's book *How to Be a Domestic Goddess* in 2000, just as I am encountering feminist literature for the first time at school, the title resonates with words we are learning like 'pedestal' and 'repression', 'binary' and 'traditional roles'. I am wary of an invitation to relish domesticity.

Nigella's use of possessive pronouns unsettles me, too. *My* chocolate cake, *my* quick pasta, *my* upmarket mushy peas. They are all declared *delicious*. To my young eyes these bold declarations about one's own cookery are uncomfortable. The possessive pronouns come across as boastful, greedy, even immodest. But eventually it dawns on me that I flinch from Nigella's on-screen display of both her own joy in her creations, and her culinary knowledge, because of internalized misogyny (when I learn what this means). And later on, I find a more radical potential in Nigella's language and food.

My   a claim to authorship, an insistence on naming

A public refusal to allow her labour in the kitchen to be exploited and plundered like some kind of natural resource, for free, and unacknowledged. She claims her own labour. Nigella often credits her sources or inspirations, but she is not afraid to name and describe her own authorial intervention into the development of a recipe that she shares with her audience. The unnamed quickly becomes forgotten and unarchived.

My   finger dipped in whipped cream

Nigella prioritizes her own pleasure; this shocks me. She tells her audience that she is cooking for her own reasons. It takes me a long time to understand that a significant aspect of my fear of Nigella has to do with her overt claim to pleasure both in her writing and on TV. She will not trivialize pleasure or pretend it's not foremost in her mind. She is telling me and you that we are worthy of pleasure and should prioritize it, too. She wants us to cook so that we can find the way to our own hearts through our stomachs. Nigella encourages readers and viewers to refuse the abjection of their bodies. Pleasure is the baseline.

These are hard messages to hear if you have been taught to unhear them.

When I watch Nigella on TV now, I see her differently than I did at high school. A journal entry from 1st December 2020 documents my attempt to describe all that is going on as Nigella serves herself a dish from her book *Cook, Eat, Repeat*:

Watching Nigella last night as she serves herself lemon and elderflower pudding, it occurs to me that she gives the viewer permission to have a body. After describing the pudding she has taken out of the oven – 'crisp and golden', 'springy', 'squidgy' – and drizzling it lavishly with elderflower cordial and lemon juice, she says, 'I'm going to give myself a bit of the corner,' as she looks down at it. Then there's a pause as she looks back at the viewer, fully facing the camera and says, 'a bit of *everything* actually.' Then she scoops three large wobbling spoons of pudding into her bowl. Not only one more spoon than the corner, but two. The repetition of serving herself more, not once, but twice, makes it a helping that is three times the size of the corner she begins with. The three servings give the performance the quality of ritual, of a spell. Each spoon of pudding strengthens the spell. It is as if Nigella banishes the cursed apparition of a disapproving look. With each spoon she rids herself of a layer of inhibition and comes closer to expressing her true appetite, her true power. Then, as if to seal the effect of her spell, Nigella pours enough double cream over the pudding to half-fill the bowl, takes it away and eats it, alone. I am reminded of Susan Sontag's 'BE BOLD BE BOLD BE BOLD!', said not once, but three times in an address to young women graduates. Three times to make it stick. The bad thing is not going to happen if you give yourself three helpings of pudding, if you let yourself exist.

Nigella encourages contemporary audiences to desire, to cook, to eat; to demand more than mere subsistence.

The choice is not between burning down the kitchen or revisiting it in a nostalgic dream-state; that is a false binary. It is bad faith to burn your grandmother's archive because she wasn't as free as you.

Cooking is a Method

(after Christina Sharpe)

Pleasure and delight in living are not peripheral to the project of liberation!

No text impresses the radical potential of cooking on me more powerfully or variously than the 'biomythography' of self-described 'black, lesbian, mother, warrior, poet,' Audre Lorde. In *Zami: A New Spelling of My Name* Lorde depicts her mother's food shopping and cooking as forms of resistance to racial oppression in the 1930s–40s Harlem of her childhood. While Linda is rarely overtly affectionate, Lorde's account of grocery shopping demonstrates her mother's insistence that her family eat beautifully –

> My mother's absolute refusal to accept butter substitutes... had us on line in front of supermarkets on bitterly cold Saturday mornings, waiting for the store to open so we could get first crack at buying our allotted quarter-pound of unrationed butter...

Throughout the war, Mother kept a mental list of all the supermarkets reachable by one bus, frequently taking only me because I could ride free. She also noted which were friendly and which were not, and long after the war ended there were meat markets and stores we never shopped in because someone in them had crossed my mother during the war over some precious scarce commodity, and my mother never forgot and rarely forgave.

Linda develops an expansive and expert geography of buying butter in New York. The travel and the cold and the queuing and hostility are preferable to eating what she would be given by the 'crushing reality' of American racism. Her daughters will have butter: through her shopping and cooking, Lorde's mother carves out a nourishing space in hostile territory. In perhaps the most detailed exposition of her mother cooking as a refusal of racism, Lorde describes a picnic. Anticipating their exclusion from segregated dining spaces on a family trip to Washington, Linda makes an exquisite picnic that attends to every conceivable desire:

My mother had roasted two chickens and cut them up into dainty bite-sized pieces. She packed slices of brown bread and butter and green pepper and carrot sticks. There were little violently yellow iced cakes with scalloped edges called 'marigolds', that came from Cushman's Bakery. There was a spice bun and rock-cakes from Newton's, the West Indian bakery across Lenox Avenue from St Mark's School, and iced tea in a wrapped mayonnaise jar. There were sweet pickles for us and dill pickles for my father, and peaches with all the fuzz still on them, individually wrapped to keep them from bruising. And, for neatness, there were piles of napkins and a little tin box with a washcloth dampened with rosewater and glycerine for wiping sticky mouths.

The picnic is a robust refusal to be denied pleasure in the way that the racist state intends. The family are not permitted to eat in the dining car on the train and when they sit down in the ice cream parlour in Washington, the white waitress will not serve them. But Linda ensures that every part of her family's bodies is exalted with the blessings of her picnic. She speaks through every detail – the 'dainty bite-sized pieces' into which she cuts the chicken; different pickles to suit different palates; the tenderness with which the peaches are handled, so that even the delicate fuzz on their skin remains intact and their soft flesh is unharmed. It is an ode to the body, causing shudders of delight. Through the picnic Linda develops a rich vision for what her family's life should be, 'creating possibility in the space of enclosure, a radical act of subsistence'. (Saidiya Hartman)

The picnic is a political imaginary that can be tasted, an opening to a reality beyond the poverty of existence to which white supremacy would consign black lives. This cook shows that liberation must give dreams earthly form. Her food demonstrates that the purpose of political struggle is to make life materially vibrant and gorgeous for each person. While Lorde's mother does not allow herself to verbally express the hope that Audre might experience fairness at school, she expresses it through the work of feeding her daughters as magnificently as she is able.

In her essay 'Poetry is Not a Luxury' (1985), Lorde emphasizes the material basis of dreaming, of poetry, of revolution, through food:

> Our children cannot dream unless they live, they cannot live unless they are nourished, and who else will feed them the real food without which their dreams will be no different from ours?

Lorde tells us that the provision of food which venerates the body and bathes it in pleasure is not a luxury: it is indivisible from political struggle. In 'Beauty is a Method' (2019), Christina Sharpe writes, 'What is beauty made of? Attentiveness whenever possible to a kind of aesthetic that escaped violence whenever possible.' Sharpe elaborates the ways in which her mother attended to the 'black aesthetic' at home, and through doing so, 'moved me from the windowsill to the world'. Oppression takes place at every scale – in the spreading of butter on bread – and the kitchen is a site from which liberation can be imagined and practised and tasted in fragments.

The Kitchen is a Weaving Room

Cooking is thinking!

I am writing an epic in which I cook the same recipe a thousand times. I will make big dick claims about the knowledge that is produced through this cooking. I am writing against the tendency for people to diminish cooking as almost the opposite of thought. Cliché is served with a side of cliché to make such work appear minor, uncomplicated or almost accidental: unworthy of critical attention. Similar thinking lies behind Sigmund Freud's suggestion in 1933 that women's only discovery in the history of civilization is the invention of weaving. But even that, Freud speculates, was probably only an imitation of nature:

> It seems that women have made few contributions to the discoveries and inventions in the history of civilization; there is, however, one technique which they may have invented – that of plaiting and weaving... Nature herself would seem to have given the model which this achievement imitates by causing

the growth at maturity of the pubic hair that conceals the genitals. The step that remained to be taken lay in making the threads adhere to one another, while on the body they stick into the skin and are only matted together.

According to Freud, weaving was invented when women plagiarized their own pubic hair – Freud's fixation on the meaning of genitals clouds his critical faculties. Having identified one single idea conceived by women in the history of civilization, Freud immediately denies them the credit for it. Here, he renders women incapable of ideation beyond the childlike imitation of their bodies.

While Freud's example may seem strange now, his (anti)analytic procedure for discussing work performed by women –

stopping short of serious enquiry
crediting authorship to the vague figure of 'Nature'
removing any element of intent/agency

is well-rehearsed. Freud's desire to undermine women's ability to have original thought displays the culturally ingrained fear of the threat posed to a patriarchal social order by women's powers of creation. Such a logic also underpins the low-paid or unpaid status of work traditionally regarded as feminine. The unfortunate effect of this pervasive way of thinking is also that people performing such work learn to deny or unsee the brilliance and potency of their own labours.

It is when I am studying the weaving trick performed by Penelope in Homer's *Odyssey* during my PhD that I begin to think differently about what I am doing in the kitchen.

The kitchen is a space for theorizing!

Penelope manipulates the patriarchal underestimation of her work as a weaver. Penelope's husband Odysseus is away for twenty years – ten years fighting in the Trojan wars and ten years sailing home – and is presumed dead. Pressure mounts for Penelope to marry again to give Ithaca a new male ruler. But she does not want to do this, so she devises a plan. Penelope promises she will choose a new husband when she finishes weaving a burial shroud for her father-in-law. This was expected of her in her contemporary culture: Penelope appears to be performing work that conforms to ancient Greek expectations for her gender.

However, under the guise of doing what is expected, Penelope does something else. For several years, she spends each night secretly unweaving what she has woven during the day. Time passes but the shroud does not grow larger and so she does not have to choose a husband. The men who want to marry Penelope are unable to understand why the weaving takes so long, because they cannot weave. Penelope works with the weaving process to make a temporal anomaly that protects her. Her weaving rooms become a space where the passing of time does not equate to the completion of the promised task. Penelope's intended result is the perpetuation of the process itself.

Penelope's epic is the story of inventing new forms of space and time (Adriana Cavarero) through a close engagement with her weaving practice. The multiplicity of intersecting threads is woven and unwoven to make a different timeline. Her weaving room becomes a parallel universe, a protected space where her body and her time are her own. Penelope develops a practice of thought impenetrable to a patriarchal gaze: a logic of unweaving. She transforms weaving from labour that takes her agency away, into a labour that gives her the power of refusal.

Penelope makes me think differently about the possibilities of cooking.

I begin to think about an epic in the kitchen, about devoting my writing to what I do there. I have the suspicion that what I am doing in the kitchen is more than I think I am doing in the kitchen. When I take stock of my life or make a narrative of it, I usually do not include recipes or my understandings of an onion. But if I brush this aside, I will brush myself aside, under the carpet, and I'll disappear into a crack in the wall like the 'I' in Ingeborg Bachmann's novel *Malina* – poof!

The movements of Penelope's hands at the loom reveal new ways of understanding space, time and productivity: what might an enquiry into cooking produce? Moments of revelation with implications far beyond the kitchen may occur through work in the kitchen. During years studying literature and theory, I do not stop to ask if the questions about language and the body that arise could be addressed through the cooking I perform every day. I echo Freud's dismissive analysis of weaving when describing my own efforts in the kitchen. I have learnt to unsee my own work and to exclude it from the frame of my own thoughts. I must work against this pervasive logic to make an account of living that does not exclude these things. I decide to find new ways to write shaped by the movements of my hands as I cook.

I decide to think with an onion, an orange, a tomato, a knife, a raging hunger. A hundred cuts with a knife *like so*, a thousand ways to use heat, and a thousand ways to change a mood.

*

When I am about to set sail, I come across a passage in the essay 'My Vocation' by Italian writer Natalia Ginzburg that reads like a blessing –

> Now I no longer wanted to write like a man because… I thought I knew a great many things about tomato sauce and even if I didn't put them in my story it helped my vocation that I knew them.
>
> (Ginzburg, trans. Dick Davis)

Ginzburg has a revelation about the form of her writing through the work of cooking tomato sauce. She realizes that she need not erase her own life to write – or, that tomato sauce is a way of doing things too. The act of writing must come from somewhere, from some life. Ginzburg has her body, her voice, her hands that have done the things they have done. She can write from tomato sauce, from children, from grief, from anger, from cleaning up sick, from care, or from anything she has done. Not necessarily about those things (she should write about whatever she likes), but from a lived position that is not made to vanish. Writing from a position that does not exist is not possible. Making tomato sauce is a position as good and as serious as any other.

Hot Red Epic

I first come across the recipe while cruising the internet at the end of my first year living alone in the city.

My student accommodation is a small room with a grey carpet and a view onto an enclosed grey roof space populated by steaming heating vents. After a few months I have made the room even less attractive than what is outside. I drop a bag of coffee onto the crowded floor and leave it there for several days, perhaps a week. It is as if a patch of earth has spontaneously appeared on the grey carpet. I am discovered standing in the grounds, stranded, when the building management come to inspect the room. Outside among other people, I conceal my squalid living habits with highly co-ordinated clothing, but I am in need of instruction.

I am seeking answers to questions I am still formulating. A relationship left over from high school disintegrates in a mess of anxiety and immature paranoia. I am excited by my new surroundings: city streets and people and cafes and shops that are walking distance from where I live. But I do not understand how to navigate them. I have come to live in London from an isolated house in a rural area with no neighbours and the casual daily encounters of shared living are novel and challenging.

I become friendly with the girl in the next-door room. She is an evangelical Christian and I have 'no religion', but we both have an enthusiasm for eating. She is fun and has a mischievous sense of humour. When I buy skinny-cut jeans, which have just begun to appear in a few shops, she makes fun of me and says they look weird (it is the tail end of the mid-2000s reign of bootcut). Sometimes, she shares plastic boxes of leftover beef rendang or papaya salad that her mother gives her after weekends at home. I have not eaten these dishes before and they give me a new way to think about salad, about sweetness and sourness, and introduce me to the almost unfathomable depths of beef rendang. She tells me about Krispy Kreme doughnuts, which have recently arrived in London. 'They are fried fresh every day in London.' I try one and am amazed at how moist how delicate how sweet. We discuss cooking and she shows me how much water to add to rice using the joints in her finger and we both agree that cuts of chicken with a bone in are more flavourful. But her social life is focussed on her evangelical church, which she attends four times a week, and I am not ripe for that kind of conversion. We have frequent conversations about our differing beliefs. I try to imagine the feeling of believing in God, but I can't. I decline invitations to play music and watch films at her church, feeling unsure about what it might require of me. I go to her Christmas carol service, hoping for singing and mince pies and to show her that there are aspects of her religious life that I can appreciate. But when I get there, the almost feverish evangelizing style and the moral condemnations issued by the pastor make me uncomfortable. He summons newcomers to come to the front of a huge congregation, admit their sins and be saved. I do not come forward.

When I prostrate myself on my bedroom floor and scream in a scene of failing teenage love I cannot hold onto, she hears through the wall and later tells me that she has prayed for me. I appreciate this as a gesture of care. She tells me she strayed from the church during her adolescence (how, I do not discover), and her family put her on a Christian medical ship for several months. When I meet her, she is back on the path of her church. After a few weeks of term, a boyfriend with an air of orthodoxy appears. He is training to be a church pastor and they are testing each other out for marriage, she tells me. We are hanging out in the corridor outside our rooms when her teenage sister visits and they tell her that her skirt is too short. This feels strange to me. My neighbour and her boyfriend tell me that women must be 'their brother's keeper'. I am confused and ask, 'Keeper from what?' They reply, 'Desire'. They ask me – 'How would you feel if a friend came to your house wearing a low-cut top in front of your boyfriend?' They try to get me to imagine circumstances in which I would turn against imaginary women for what they wear. My feeling that we cannot go much further together is sealed by a conversation in which she tells me about gay conversion therapy. I have not heard of it before and feel a slow creep of horror as I understand what she is telling me. Their endeavour to live out such narrow interpretations of the Bible is unappealing – a hermeneutics so weighted against desiring bodies.

Cooking and eating offer more interesting lessons.

A Neapolitan student along the corridor from me eats the same breakfast every day: a chocolate biscuit spread with Nutella, an espresso and a cigarette. He makes tomato sauce by frying a peeled garlic clove in olive oil and then removing the clove and then adding smooth passata, which I have not encountered before. He tells me that he does this so that the garlic flavours the oil. He also makes a dish of Heinz baked beans mixed with pasta and a beef burger on top. I introduce him to Krispy Kreme doughnuts, which he adores. On one joyful occasion, he eats six of their glazed ring doughnuts in quick succession. He is older than me, in his early twenties, and at home in Italy he lives with his parents and his mother cooks for him and his younger brother. He is particular about how various things should be done. He teaches me the phrase-gesture vaffanculo! (*fuck you!*), emphasizing the combination of hand and body movements that should accompany the word, the meaning of which changes with each physical performance.

He introduces me to a cafe near our accommodation where I eat sandwiches made from large loaves of ciabatta bread with mortadella, cheese, salad and artichoke hearts that the owner dresses fastidiously with a vinegary herb mixture using a teaspoon from a little bowl. I eat parmigiana di melanzane, a sea of melted cheese, fried aubergines and tomato sauce that they serve with a small wicker basket of bread lined with a paper napkin, also seasoned with the vinegary herb dressing. The owner speaks to me in Italian I can barely understand, but never abandons me for bad pronunciation. Occasionally, I join my friend to watch Napoli play football in the basement of the cafe. We are handed a Parma ham sandwich and a bottle of cold beer as we file down the narrow stairs to watch the game on five or six differently sized TVs amidst clouds of cigarette smoke and enthusiastic swearing.

In an experiment with pleasure, I go and buy a coffee and a takeaway box of profiteroles in the late afternoon. When ordering the coffee on my own, I think carefully about the correct coffee to have from observing other people in the cafe, and also recall a text we studied at school in which a travel writer (I think Paul Theroux) says that it is incorrect to have a cappuccino at any time of day other than breakfast in Italy, so I buy an espresso. It is bracingly bitter and I am not sure that I enjoy the taste, but I enjoy feeling like I am doing the right thing. The profiteroles are served out of a disposable foil tray and are submerged in a thickened sweet cream with a touch of cocoa. They are different from the version I once cooked at home with dark chocolate and whipped cream. I have never lived in a city. I have never lived a convenient walking distance from a shop or a cafe or a restaurant, I have never even lived near people outside my immediate family. The interactions required to buy the profiteroles are overwhelming at first, an unfamiliar public performance.

The cafe is narrow and long and dimly lit with small chrome tables and chairs. TVs are showing different Italian stations, there is a pile of pink Italian newspapers and middle-aged Italian men drink coffee and chat. An open refrigerator hums and displays Italian branded soft drinks, Coca-Cola and beer. The menu is up on three chalkboards in Italian with English underneath. Subheadings divide menu choices into Panini Italiani, Hot Food, Large Salads, Basic Rolls, Dolci, Breakfasts and Hot Drinks, with different prices for eat-in and takeaway, reflecting the tax on eating in. Football scarves, strips, balls and other memorabilia from teams in Serie A, the Italian football league, hang from the ceiling. Young children and extended family wander in and out from behind the counter. The owner, who has a gentle manner even when it's very busy, cuts bread, watches the queue, dresses his sandwiches, cares for his children. In the cafe I encounter new words and gestures and the distinct ways that each dish is prepared and served.

Through my Neapolitan neighbour I meet some of the other visiting Italian students in my block, including a man from Florence, who is known to be the best cook among the Italians and is nominated their chef. He smokes a lot of weed and claims to be a descendant of the Medici dynasty, with credible evidence. He discusses the correct amount of onion to add to pasta sauces with great passion. The excesses of undercooked and roughly cut onion in sauces made by British students horrify him. His body contracts as he explains how much (how little) he would add – a quarter of an onion, very finely diced, a half, *absolute maximum.*

One night as I walk through the communal dining area, the Italian students invite me to join them and eat his pasta. There are around ten people at the table, and they move up to make space for me. The pasta is divided to allow me to eat, too. The Florentine has made a sauce from a little diced salmon and a little cream and a little onion, cooked until sweet. The richly flavoured sauce just coats the strands of pasta and there are a few flakes of salmon in each bowl, enough to give sustenance and delight to every person around the table.

*

When I first find the recipe that I will cook a thousand times, I am reminded of the Florentine's focus on each ingredient as he makes his sauce – the effects each one can have, what it might become, how it could change the whole.

the special taste depends largely
on the way ____ is handled

I have never met the person who wrote the recipe, but it is recommended to me on a newspaper website by a cook who has been recommended to me by another cook, whose judgement I trust because I have tasted her food. The route to the recipe is made by tongues.

It is by far the cheapest and easiest recipe in a feature about famous chefs' favourite recipes, but it is precise in ways I do not expect.

During my first performance of the recipe, I have a revelation about ingredients, or vegetables: they are *things*. I must learn to watch them closely, ready to accommodate their whims, which are not human.

The recipe is a method for responding to things. Things have agency in many directions. Like words, they have histories and contexts, but when I perform the recipe, things become other things in a messier transformation than words in a sentence. They spatter my shirt red.

The recipe is a text that can produce spattering because it was spattering before it was language. Language is only a holding pattern for the recipe – not its origin, nor its terminus.

Spattering is not mentioned in the recipe. The text does not anticipate the liveliness of the process it describes, which spatters wildly. The substance in the pan trespasses beyond its linguistic boundary, making marks, or mark-making on my shirt, the wall, the dry surface of whatever book is close by. There is always *more*. There is more than has been recorded in the text and there will be more again. Things will be hotter and redder. There will be spattering.

In some ways the recipe text gives me no clue about what is to come. This is hard to forgive. But after cooking it a thousand times, the recipe turns out to be Good Enough. It holds me and it survives my many attempts to destroy it. (D.W. Winnicott)

The second, third, fourth time I make the recipe I follow the instructions as precisely as I can, reverent and still wonderstruck by the transformation of matter in which I am a participant.

My body is changed by the recipe –

after tasting it, I see flavour differently, which means I see *things* differently, because flavour is a quality of things, or can be. And it's not seeing, it's tasting, but it's a tasting that inaugurates a different relationship to things, a new method of perceiving. It is not only the surface I am looking at; I am learning to see *into* things, seeking the dimension of Being that is flavour. There are so many possibilities. Each time I encounter the same thing, the same ingredient, I find that it's different again, again, different again, so the recipe is always a method for seeking.

turn the heat down to very low

On the eighth time of making the recipe I do not add fresh herbs at the end because I have run out of money. The herbs cost more than the rest of the ingredients put together in the small urban supermarket near where I live. It is less fragrant but still intense; it tastes redder.

For my twelfth performance, several months later, I am exhausted from working until 3 a.m. in a pub and I have missed the closing time of the last pizza place that delivers in south London. I decide to free-pour the oil instead of measuring it spoon by spoon. Even while tired I feel the frisson of resistance to the text's specificity and have a small conversation in my head with the author of the recipe where I explain that even though I have not measured the oil, it's probably almost the same.

For the twenty-first performance I change the preparation of the garlic and I don't slice it *very thinly* as the recipe instructs. Instead, imitating the movements of a man I have recently met, I crush it and keep crushing it and crushing with a knife until it is almost a paste, which turns out to be quite difficult and annoying to do, and the taste is different. My tired wrists know the extent of my deviation from the method. The change in method means I can no longer see when the garlic *becomes coloured a pale gold* as the recipe text directs, so I turn to my nose for navigational purposes. This different way of preparing garlic is brought on by a kind of blindness called desire, which drives me off my intended course.

Cutting and slicing is not a matter of dividing one thing into smaller fractions of the same thing; after cutting, it is not the same thing. In Harold McGee's encyclopaedia of kitchen science, I read that in the case of garlic and other alliums, when cells are cut, an enzyme trigger is released that interacts with chemical ammunition to produce a pungent sulphurous molecule designed to deter animals from eating them. The taste which attracts us should read as poison. The enzyme reaction in garlic produces a hundredfold higher concentration of molecules than other alliums. Slicing, pounding and crushing do not only change the physical shape of a garlic clove into smaller pieces. Each method alters the very chemistry, the very Being of the clove in a different way. The clove cannot be reassembled or returned to the clove it once was. Form and structure is a matter of Being, too.

During the thirtieth performance I enthusiastically tell a new housemate (the first I have had) what the recipe has taught me about the thermodynamics of oil. On a low heat oil rises slowly until it *floats free*, gleaming and tinted red. The oil cooks the garlic gently and circulates its sweetness. Stirring too vigorously can emulsify the oil with other liquids in the pan and prevent it from moving in this special way.

In the fortieth performance I am cooking for someone who likes capers and chilli and so I add capers and chilli flakes. Even though I know that capers are not integral to the recipe and that they are not written in the recipe and

54

that this addition in some ways violates the principles of the recipe, when we eat, we can taste capers and heat and that is what they wanted. Capers are a challenge for my childish palate because it is not long since I left home, and my mother does not like capers and does not put them in her cooking.

The year I begin cooking the recipe is the year I go to a famous hairdressing school and let an experimental stylist cut off all my hair. They do not charge a fee, and I am in need of a new direction, an escape route from my body which has begun to feel altogether too constricting. *Directional* is what they call their haircuts – just what I need! The experimental hairdresser is an intense East Londoner in her forties and deeply focussed on her art. My hair becomes the medium with which she works to produce a new cut, a new dish. She tends to my hair in the way that the recipe encourages me to tend to ingredients, responding to their qualities, their potential for trans-formation. She likes that the hairs on my head are fine but abundant so she can create volume and achieve great height without the weight of the hair causing collapse. She describes this to audiences who are watching her and writing down the recipe, planning to bring these techniques to their home salons, like a cookery demonstration.

All that is required of me when she cuts my hair is to sit still for hours and hours, sometimes up to eight hours. My phone gets no signal in the basement salon, and I let my mind wander. The hairdresser does not require me to speak, or to say 'I'; she just needs me to sit, silent and unmoving. It is very freeing to be this way. I become a body without words, present only as a medium, willingly manipulated. I let her cut my hair again and again, sometimes on a stage while someone talks and points at my head, sometimes in a teaching salon. But even when on stage, I am not required to be a subject. It takes hours of concentration for her to produce brave new shapes with my hair using scissors, combs, heat and air. She collaborates with colourists who participate in constructing the haircuts. They spend hours painting my hair and folding it up in foil and when they unwrap it, vibrant abstract images have appeared on my head. Each colour changes how the light will filter through the manifold textures she has produced. She makes smooth curves or pointillist stubble or rough clashing waves that reach great crescendos; long single strands and thick blocks refract light at different frequencies. I am struck when the hairdresser refers to my hair as 'virgin' on stage during a demonstration. She means undyed, but the erotic dimension of our strange relationship does not escape me. She appears in several dreams.

After the first cut with the experimental hairdresser, I find I can breathe more easily, and more easily still each time after that. I did not grow up at a time when popular culture accepted that people should have autonomy over their appearance. *What Not to Wear* is the mantra we were encouraged to repeat to ourselves, learnt from the wildly popular BBC television series that launched in 2001, when I was fifteen. Body parts including legs and arms and stomachs, body hair, displays of 'masculine muscles', unfeminine haircuts and, above all, fat are prodded and condemned by presenters on the violently normative and fatphobic TV show. When I let the stylist experiment with my hair, I begin to feel released from something constraining and oppressive. Like the recipe, the haircuts change the relationship between words and things for me. The experimental hairdresser gives me the knowledge that I can remake my body, again and again. It becomes a space for play, exploration and deviation.

Each time I cook the recipe differently, my hair is different too –

There is the time I make the recipe after my long brown hair has been cut into an asymmetric shape with a shaved side, a bob on the other side and a thin 'veil' of hair at the back.

Two weeks later they have dyed my hair dark auburn and black and purple at the front.

Several months after that I cook with deep pink hair with a pale pink fringe and black marks drawn onto my face.

Then it becomes bright red and a spherical bob with a slight asymmetry, after Vidal Sassoon.

The people I have recently moved in with love comic books and cosplay and make-up and Zelda and making their own porn and horror films and foxes and Halloween parties and watching all of *Buffy the Vampire Slayer* from start to finish and I love them and take out a standing order at a comic book shop too. They like the hairstyles I come home with, whatever they are, and love whatever clothes I wear and whatever make-up I try and will come and queue with me for whatever obnoxious club night with a 'no look no entry' policy that I am obsessed with. They let me cook excitable meals for them even though sometimes I fill the house with smoke or spray it with mushroom soup when the blender explodes; I teach them the recipe.

The trick is to slow-cook

For the seventieth performance my anxiety causes me to turn the heat up too high. I hurry things. I have retreated into myself and fail to keep faith with the ingredients. I interfere and force my will on the ingredients and forget that it is a collaboration. The excess heat I apply has the effect of a weapon; it is wounding. The flavour at the end lacks sweetness and depth and I have to repair the dish, inventing ways to accommodate my impatience. The damage I visit upon the ingredients must be repaired with new ingredients: *I add sugar and a half teaspoon of vinegar.*

When I think about performing the recipe I think about the movements of subatomic particles or the orbits of moons and planets, there is a physics to it. The recipe introduces me to principles of touch, knifework, heat and time. The temporality of white becoming gold in oil. I must be careful about how I move my hands, the interventions they make can be significant, they are always in relation. In the study of electrons nothing is ignored because everything can have an effect, even looking. The proverb 'a watched pot never boils' was taken up by physicists trying to find ways to describe the behaviour of quantum particles. 'Watched pot behaviour' is another term for the Zeno effect in quantum physics, whereby frequent measurement inhibits the process being observed from actually taking place. Sometimes my anxiety or impatience causes me to take the pan off the heat too soon.

Cooking often hovers at the fringes of serious thought. I see it used as metaphor in philosophical texts, invoked in introductory paragraphs, deployed to convey the complexity of processes that are not cooking. But I find I need to draw on all available resources to articulate the complexity of the recipe. After ten years or more of experimentation I have not exhausted its possibilities; I have not found a limit for what the recipe can teach me about being in the world.

The recipe is a method of navigation, a method for seeing or seeking what is beyond me.

The recipe makes a space in my life where time does not pass but accumulates as a hot red sea full of feeling, good and bad.

The month before I move to Berlin to study and work, I perform the recipe and my hair is even shorter and red with a blue and blonde fringe; blue quickly fades to grey.

For the first performance of the recipe in Berlin my hair is white blonde and I have painted the top half of my face pink, I am drunk, and I play Giorgio Moroder, whose music I have recently started listening to. I put my favourite apron over my clothes; it is checked green and orange and is made from pliable cotton and I pull it tight. In this apron I orchestrate many large meals. I become a conductor of chopping and frying and drinking and dancing.

For the third performance of the recipe in Berlin my hair is still white blonde. I am wearing blue lipstick with dark blue glitter over the top, affixed with lip gloss, and dramatic black eyebrows painted much higher than my own on my forehead, black eyeliner, a drawn-on beauty spot and a blue leotard. The more artificial I look the better it feels, being not essentially anything. At 3 a.m. I go to the club Berghain with my friends and we queue in the snow and then dance to pounding techno until 11 a.m., which counts as an early bedtime for many attendees.

When I am not in nightclubs or cooking in the apartment, I wander the city alone wearing large headphones. The headphones make a space for me that is insulated from social interactions. Most nights when I am not out I wake up at 4 or 5 a.m. in a panicked alcohol sweat and call the very patient person I am seeing long-distance in the UK. Apart from my Norwegian flatmate with whom I spend most of my time, a philosophy graduate I recognize in a nightclub from a London library, the owner of the fashion store I work in and a customer whom I befriend, the only people I speak to are those with few enough boundaries to make it past my headphones.

The philosophy graduate from Scotland picks the meat from a chicken I have cooked and talks about an ex-girlfriend and Throbbing Gristle and who he wants to fuck now – he's sure they'll be out this week. When we have drunk everything in the flat we leave to be in the perfect and blessed light of Berlin nightclubs where I dance until the make-up runs down my face. A tall and beautiful man called Vladimir is on the door of the club that becomes like home for a short, sweet while. Peaches sings *fuck the pain away* from a podium with her pubic hair spewing gloriously from her sequinned leotard, free blue packs of Gauloises cigarettes are handed out to everyone. A French man with a moustache called Charlie Le Mindu is shaving heads for fifteen euros in the basement. We exit at 4 a.m. to eat a kebab, and then go back in to dance again, or perhaps onwards to Berghain. Every dance floor is an ecstatic exploration of our desires, our bodies.

The two hundredth time I make the recipe is a kind of madness. Cooking becomes a social support I lean on too heavily. A German teenager in my literature class at the university manages to strike up a conversation, declaring her admiration for my tight red jeans. Unprepared and taken aback, I give a freakish and exaggerated performance of social courtesy and promise to cook a meal for all her friends for her birthday at my apartment without asking my flatmates. She is local and lives with her parents and treats the occasion as a chance to go wild. I feel hysterical as I serve food to dozens of people I have never met who flood the apartment, play music I don't like and intrude on my flatmates' private space. I find out that I do not like the girl whose birthday party I am hosting, that I do not know her at all; we do not really speak again after that night. Even worse, I make a fatal substitution in the recipe, not anticipating how differently the ingredient would behave. The thought of all these strangers eating the manic, bad dish haunts me painfully.

When the temperature is so low that the cold burns my face I buy a bag of oranges from Lidl. I take one out. It is an orange against drinking and against the lost feeling I can't shake. I buy the webbed bag of fruit as a tonic, as a way of following advice that I have not received for years. It is a way of following my mother's advice even if it has never been given, a dream of good advice, which I plan to absorb with each segment. I peel the orange hopefully, like it will be a doctor, an oracle, a cure, but when I gaze full of hope into the wet orange flesh it moves. The orange flesh moves, wriggles and is alive and I am not hallucinating. The orange is full of maggot larvae. The oranges are the birthplace of decay whose life was throbbing evidence against mine and I scream and throw it against the wall in the kitchen and it splats and sprays orange juice and larvae all over, running into each other in drips down the wall. I have never been more shocked. I eat no more oranges that winter.

In London again I make the recipe and my hair is a short bowl cut, dyed deep burgundy red.

Then I dye it black and shave an undercut, too. When I cook, as when I walk around the city, I wear a long, black blazer over buttoned-up shirts with black platform boots. My lipstick is bright orange or blue or black or purple, any colour but red.

However, while I love clothes and make-up, I am beginning to use them like a carapace, a hard shell to protect myself from other people, from the vulnerability of intimacy. I set too much store by appearances and control mine too tightly.

Cooking is the tool I use to draw close to other people, though closeness makes me anxious. Cooking is how I manage closeness. Sometimes it can go wrong, like the stranger's birthday party in Berlin. Cooking for someone is not always an appropriate response to meeting them.

But sometimes, it's OK.

For the two hundred and fortieth performance, four years after I first made the recipe, I make it for you:

> at least there is that *You*, which is every beloved, which constitutes itself across difference and species and the whole of life. *You* is eros and caritas all mixed up in a word. It is also the stranger who any of us might be, and in that the only law is probably love, and that the violation of life anywhere is the violation of life everywhere, and in that no one is free until everyone is, *You* is what everything in the world is staked on, including yourself. _(Anne Boyer)

You teach me about cooking for every other Other; you teach me about 'that *You*'.

You are almost a stranger – we haven't known each other long – but I stake myself on cooking for you.

You tell me that some ingredients disagree with you, there are certain things you cannot eat, but you can eat everything in the recipe. So I make it for you once, and you love it, and then I make it for you a hundred times.

Years later you say you would like to eat the recipe as your last meal, and that sometimes when we are apart, you type my first name and the title of the recipe into an internet search, which of course doesn't turn up anything useful.

When I am thinking about what to cook for you, I return

to the recipe as a meditative practice, to the beginning of what I know you can eat. Your appetite changes the recipe over time; I ask what else you want, and I change the recipe to make something that is new and also the same.

For the three hundred and sixty-fifth performance of the recipe I add things that make it sweet and sour and spiced and serve it with lamb patties to evoke a meal we ate with our friends by a river several summers before. Now we are in the city and it is not warm, but when we eat that evening, we are drunk by the river again.

Here again here again here again,
the recipe becomes an ensemble performance.

Writing recipes for you is the beginning of my writing. I begin writing so you will have recipes when you need them – when I am not there. In periods when I stop writing recipes, which is also when I have felt most distant from myself, most anxious, you ask me to write again and say that you miss it. So, I begin again. I am able to do very little without being asked, unable to see a reason why. What purpose would it serve? Your appetite, your asking summons a subject again and again, often just as it is – as I am – fading.

When we do not see each other often and live in different places, I cook a dish for you even though you are not there and have not asked, so that I can write down the new recipe and send it to you.

The original wording of the recipe, which I have not read in many years, recedes in my mind although all of my movements and decisions are shaped by it and are in relation to it, even as they are different.

For the four hundred and fifty-first performance I make the recipe then I use it as the basis for a different dish for two women. Both are hot. There is sexual tension in circulation that I cannot yet articulate. I am in a bad relationship with a man who lives far away, and I am unhappy. I sublimate my feelings into cooking. We eat and then squash together on a sofa to watch a trippy American TV series, the room shimmering with desire. I write a recipe for the dish during the first month of writing down recipes on a website I have made.

The five hundred and third performance of the recipe is wretched. I barely want to eat the dish. I am so paralysed by the fear of failure that writing even one word of my PhD makes it difficult to breathe. I struggle for several hours to get off the sofa before I can cook. I am only able to get off the sofa and cook because a friend rings me and tells me to do so. A ball of sadness and anxiety burns in my torso, making it difficult to taste my food.

I have the feeling that the balance between words and things is off, that words have been mapped onto the world, constraining its wild potential into a narrow use of language. The asymmetry of the word-world relationship bothers me like a physical irritation. For example, the word 'woman', about which I can't say more than *it doesn't sit right with me*. It feels like a closed semantic circuit limiting the way I walk, move my hands and my face, use my voice. I want to crack it open, refuse it. I have the urgent desire to sever the bond between the word and my body, my life. What else might I become?

While studying literature and philosophy we look closely at language and its effects, what it does. I find that words have been used like maps to impose order from above. Sometimes writers use language to make it seem like certain forms of knowledge are not knowledge at all, or to make it seem like certain forms of life are not really life. The forms of knowledge and of life that are diminished in the texts we study are almost always attributed to women. In my experience of higher education, conversations about what counts as 'serious thought' situate the recipe outside of the space of intellectual enquiry. When it comes to cooking, the academy is at sea.

But I have also been blind to my own knowledge-making practices, to my own research. I have not seen the knowledge that the recipe gives me as part of 'what I know'.

The six hundred and fiftieth time I make the recipe I make a space in the sauce halfway through cooking and break in two eggs because it is the morning, and in the morning by this point in my mid-twenties, I eat eggs for breakfast. I eat eggs for breakfast because several years ago I lived in Berlin with people who ate eggs for breakfast. Imitating the egg-eating of the people I lived with in Berlin enables me slowly to overcome a childhood fear and dislike of eggs.

I discover that many people have a strong feeling of connection with eggs; eggs are a good, even inexhaustible, topic for conversation.

Someone I meet from a dating website tells me about the American food writer M.F.K. Fisher. I read her book *How to Cook a Wolf* and admire the thought: 'Probably one of the most private things in the world is an egg until it is broken.'

Fisher continues,

> Until then, you would think its secrets are its own, hidden behind the impassive beautiful curvings of its shell, white or brown or speckled. It emerges full-formed, almost painlessly (The *egg* may not be bothered, but nine years and two daughters after writing this I wonder somewhat more about the *hen*. I wrote, perhaps, too glibly.) from the hen. It lies without thought in the straw, and unless there is a thunderstorm or a sharp rise in temperature it stays fresh enough to please the human palate for several days.

I like Fisher's concern for the hen who lays the eggs. Fisher thinks of the egg-worker.

There is a long period when, channelling my newfound delight in egg-eating, I crack eggs into the pan. The egg version of the recipe develops its own life. I find that I can give ten people breakfast at once by baking large serving dishes or make a lunch for one friend to eat with bread.

At one point I begin, then abandon an essay about the TV detective Columbo and eggs, in which I theorize that Columbo is an egg.

In the episode 'Murder by the Book', directed by Steven Spielberg, Columbo wears his egg-shell-coloured raincoat and makes an omelette in a suspect's kitchen. He moves manically round the room, muttering a recipe to himself – 'cheese, and onions and, um, butter, cheese and onions, and, err, I need something to, ah, grate the cheese' – and cracks eggs until the suspect becomes an egg and cracks too and brings the conversation back to the crime, revealing herself. In other episodes, Columbo produces a hard-boiled (ha ha) egg from his raincoat pocket to eat for breakfast, which he says he prefers with salt. Sometimes he carries a salt shaker in the pockets of his coat. The ordinary but uncanny intimacy brokered by the eggs affects the suspects much like the presence of Columbo. There is an inevitability to the cracking of an egg. If you see it, you know it will be cracked; they see him break the egg on the tyre iron, they know they will be cracked too. Columbo remains unknown and uncracked in his eggshell raincoat. He is the egg who will crack you. He uses eggs to gesture to his inner life, telling stories about a wife we never meet while remaining 'the most private thing in the world'. The suspects are eggs, Columbo is an egg, the eggs are eggs…

… I am rapidly losing control of the narrative.

Eggs provoke speculation that spirals out of control.

I make the egg version of the recipe all over the place and for so many people and I change the egg recipe, too. I add:

potatoes
onion
peppers
sausage
spiced sausage
lardons
coriander
spinach
and garnish with
garlic yogurt
spiced butter
Turkish chilli flakes
fresh herbs
and more I cannot remember.

Finally, the egg dish becomes as overwrought as a late Victorian house with too many turrets.

The eight hundred and ninetieth time, I make the recipe because I have nothing else in the cupboard and I have run out of money. I am bored of it, and I don't want to eat it; I resent it.

The recipe has spattered my clothes and the wall and cookbooks and my computer; it has also spattered other books. Sometimes I am cooking because I am turning away from my PhD about a rewriting of the *Odyssey* by German poet Barbara Köhler. Often, I am not waving but drowning. As part of my study, I read *Dialectic of Enlightenment* (1944) by German philosophers Theodor Adorno and Max Horkheimer. In it, they present Odysseus's epic journey and the challenges he overcomes as an allegory for the development of the 'rational' subject. In Odysseus's attempts to defeat various feminine, monstrous and natural Others on his journey, Adorno and Horkheimer see a subject who wants to master the 'uncivilized' aspects of life. Odysseus reaches the ironic conclusion that the greatest threat to life is the vital quality of embodied life itself, which is too emotional and too unreliable to be predicted and controlled.

Life is too much like spattering! Not enough like language!

In the eight hundredth performance of the recipe, I use butter instead of oil. It smells sweet and musky instead of grassy and peppery and I do it because I want to feel rich and erotic and it works. I have a new friend who makes it in this way, and I imitate her gestures. Through imitating her gestures, I find out something new about flavour that reading the recipe text alone does not reveal.

Odysseus is a logocentrist; he favours 'language or words to the exclusion or detriment of the matters to which they refer'. (Oxford English Dictionary) When he encounters the Sirens, creatures who are half-bird, half-woman, Odysseus wants to hear their song because it contains knowledge of everything that has happened on the earth. He wants to have the Sirens' knowledge for himself, but he wants it without hazarding his body. As he approaches the Sirens, Odysseus ties himself to the mast of his ship and blocks his rowers' ears with wax, hoping to listen and survive. He will not put his skin in the game. He listens to their song from afar and the rowers keep the ship moving past.

In the nine hundred and twenty-first performance, a decade after the first, I leave out the garlic and add anchovies and rosemary or *rosmarinus* or 'dew of the sea', and then at the end I add double cream because I want to be overtaken by silken intensity and fragrance, a kind of transcendence, and that is what I feel. In a moment of ecstasy as its flavour courses through my body, I call the recipe a goddess.

The knowledge of all things is embedded in the effects of the Sirens' song on the listener's body. Sailors are physically drawn to the Sirens when they sing, and therein lies the danger. But when Odysseus ties his body to the mast of the boat and sails by without moving closer, he breaks the connection between their song and the body of the listener. The Sirens' words lose their bond to the physical world when Odysseus seizes their knowledge and disregards the presence it commands. To avoid the danger of his own desire Odysseus holds the world at arm's length and language 'begins to pass over into designation…' (Adorno and Horkheimer, trans Jephcott) Knowing becomes looking and pointing from a distance.

I realize that in the kitchen I am grappling with the same questions as in my academic study. When I cook the recipe, I experience the difference between the knowledge promised by language, and the unboundedness of embodiment, which is both richer and more dangerous that the text can convey. And sometimes, like Odysseus, I distance myself from other people, from desire, from intimacy. How much should I hazard? Sometimes I want more control than is possible, so I hide rather than risk the vulnerability of proximity.

Can I know a recipe without cooking it?

The more I think about it, the more I think Odysseus is tricking himself. The Sirens' song is information that is known through an ecstatic collision of words and bodies. It is an invitation to a way of knowing that includes the emergent liveliness of things. Even though he extracts the Sirens' language, Odysseus cannot receive the knowledge contained in their song because he does not partake of it with his body. By refusing to accept the song as a physical event, Odysseus can only access an abstract version of what it imparts. It is as if Odysseus reads the recipe text but never cooks it. For the Sirens, knowledge is not separable from the song, from singing. I cannot know the recipe text until I cook it.

Cooking by the recipe a thousand times and more gives me this insight into language and its relation to living things.

A recipe that is 'distanced from any particular content which fulfils it' (Adorno and Horkheimer, trans Jephcott) is a joke, is irrational, because it feeds no body.

A recipe that feeds nobody has no future.

Before the recipe was a text it was written by the body: it was cooked. The recipe bears the traces of its corporeal origins by remaining in the service of the body. Without a body (and bodies, things, ingredients) a recipe text makes no sense.

The ethics of the recipe text arise from its proximity to life, to hungry bodies.

The recipe is always gathering life into itself, gathering words and things and people together, again and again. Rolled-up sleeves. How will life continue? Like this, like this, here and there and then and now.

Thinking about the many realities that have unfolded through the scant language of the recipe, I can see words as capacious again, as shifting over time through being cooked again, again, again, differently.

The recipe shows me time as material change. The recipe establishes a correspondence between material change and language, between time and language.

The recipe means that time is no longer divisible like empty abstract space. (Bergson via Deleuze)

The recipe intends life: language surviving through the body which eats with a different appetite each day.

There is the body and bodies who have produced the recipe and the bodies that it serves, a recipe is a text that is *for*, for the pleasure of *You*, you, them.

The recipe only returns at the request of the body.

The recipe serves at the pleasure of the body.

The recipe text will always be specific, or be made specific, and is in dialogue with specific appetites. The recipe is rewritten by the people to whom it attends.

Descriptions of people cooking always move me so much, I think this is why.

In the philosophy and theory I study, the movement of life into language appears again and again as a kind of hollowing out, a loss. A loss of the kind that Odysseus both suffers and inflicts. I do not find a way beyond this impasse until I begin to think through the recipe, until I devote myself to thinking with it. The recipe offers something else; not a nothing at the end of writing, but life returned to language a thousand times over.

The recipe is my epic (and yours too). The recipe is the ship and the hot red sea. In the recipe epic life is measured in spoons of sauce. Again and again the recipe brings me 'that *You*' (Boyer) who is also every you in particular. *You* are the beginning of my writing, of my epic.

*

The thousandth performance of the recipe takes place after speaking to you on the phone.

You tell me you feel anxious and panicky. We have been living through a global pandemic for six months and I have not seen you in person for almost a year. By chance you will be close by at the weekend to see your mother, who is not well. I measure out the oil spoon by spoon as I have not done for several years and follow the written instructions as precisely as I am able. My hands are shaky, and I hold onto the recipe text to navigate. I make double quantities, because I feel like that is what is needed and pour it into a glass jar which I have sterilized. I carry the tomato sauce with me as I travel to meet you. When I hand it to you your partner says, Oh, is that some kind of special sauce? I say, I just know that you like it. Later on, you tell me that I have given you love in the form of tomato sauce.

I cook the sauce hundreds of times with the thought that I might be making you; then I realize that you have made me.

A paradox: the recipe is the ship and the hot red sea
                    the structure that holds me and
                                      the sea that
                                  breaks it apart

                         the recipe cannot be located
                         cannot be seen from a distance
                         no external position is possible

                                         the recipe is
                          within and without the storm
                                     at the same time

                                   the ribs of the recipe,
                                              the bark
                                    is taking on water

              hot salt water streams down my chest
                  it must be sliced very thinly,
              is an effective method for bailing out

                  when the oil floats free
              we eat red and hot and pale gold
    colours we cannot see but swim through.

78

Tracing the Sauce Text

During the ten years in which I cook the recipe, I spend a lot of time in the library. I am often reading about the 'reception' of the *Odyssey*. The books here are in a different state from my cookery books. They are not spattered with oil. The recipes I use the most have the most spattering on them. I dart between the printed page and the stove, hastily flicking through to refind my place with hands covered in the ingredients with which I work. Some pages are stuck together. As I search in the online library catalogue for more books on 'reception', I notice that the keys on my laptop are sticking from cooking while reading a recipe from its screen a week ago.

It is quiet in the library, people are sitting in chairs quietly, there is no music. The temperature and the light levels are stable, it is almost as if time is not passing. No liquids are permitted in case of spillages. In the kitchen the atmosphere is changeable. I open the window to let out smoke from grilled vegetables, or sneeze from spices in the air, or shield myself from a frying egg that is spitting hot fat onto all that surrounds it. There are the sounds of cooking, or music on the radio, or talking, or all of these things at once.

'Reception' is how classical texts like the *Odyssey* are read, translated, repurposed and rewritten by different people up to the present moment. Reception studies struggled to gain legitimacy in the field of classics because it does not principally concern itself with the 'original' versions of texts. It is a discipline in which the focus might be on how an ancient text has been reimagined by writers from working-class backgrounds or writers of colour or women – groups historically (and still) excluded from classical studies. For example, playwright Suzan-Lori Parks rewrote the *Odyssey* as *Father Comes Home from the Wars*, an epic drama about an enslaved man called Hero/Ulysses who goes to fight in the American Civil War. Parks's play is also a commentary on the issues facing Black Americans at the time of writing (2014); it 'swoops, leaps, dives and soars… reimagining a turbulent turning point in American history through a cockeyed contemporary lens'. (Charles Isherwood)

Reception studies acknowledges the partial status of the 'original' and treats the text as something that is still effectively in the process of being written. To those who regard themselves as guardians of the unspattered so-called original, reception studies threatens the source of their power.

In the library, I begin to think about how the study of reception is like a study of spattering from the pan: how people have received and translated a text into their lives. Likewise, when I am back in the kitchen stirring the sauce, I begin to think about how cooking is an act of reception. The reception of the recipe is the cooking and eating of it: how absurd to disregard that!

My 'reception' of the recipe – my intervention into the tradition of recipe reception – is to translate text into food. Each time I cook the recipe I produce a new translation of the text. I translate the recipe from the medium of language into the spattering physicality of the ingredients. Like different translations of the *Odyssey*, my translations of the recipe vary in accordance with the historical moment. I might make shortcuts because I am tired from work, or changes based on the influence of another person's appetite, or additions that taste right on a particular day: cooking it like *this* to feel like *that*.

Reception is a nice and accommodating word; I like it. It is a space and an occasion to receive visitors. It also shares a root with the word 'recipe', which in older cookery books is written as 'receipt'. The recipe is capacious and roomy and allows those who enter to change it. I cook the recipe a thousand times or more and other people cook it a thousand times or more too. The recipe spreads around like sauce. It is an epic without a hero. Broad reception enriches rather than impoverishes the recipe by giving many hands powers of transformation. The recipe can show us the potency of language that is on the brink of translation into life.

When is the recipe?

Where is the recipe?

No return to the 'original' recipe is possible because its original form has been eaten. In the form of a written text, the recipe itself is already a 'translation' from a physical form. It has been translated into language from a source text – from a hot red sauce text. Unlike an ancient scroll, however, the sauce cannot be found in a tomb. Someone ate it, sometime earlier, somewhere. Despite the feeling of stability that a printed text inspires, it is only one annotation, a receipt of one instance of the recipe being cooked. The recipe is an altogether more slippery entity.

The residue of the original recipe is now said to feed the great-great-great-great-great-grandchildren of the worms who were contemporaries of the cook.

The recipe is pure reception. It is always in many places at once: in a book with spattered pages, on a website, in someone's memory or half-memory, on a shopping list, simmering in a pan or in the muscles of someone who has cooked it many times. It is in the composition of the sauce, and it is in the text; it cannot be definitively located in one place. This frustrates those who seek to identify and venerate the original version of the recipe.

Does knowledge exist if you cannot find its beginning?

The recipe is a philological nightmare! But knowing this – and taking on the guise of a classical archaeologist – I seek out earlier printed versions of the recipe that I first encountered. I want to see how they are different. I know it is a fool's errand to search for an 'original', but I go anyway to see what I find en route.

＊

The text of the tomato sauce recipe that becomes the subject of my epic, that I find online on the *Guardian* website in their feature on famous chefs' favourite recipes, is written by Ruth Rogers. She is co-founder and chef at the famous River Cafe restaurant in London. Here is the text of the recipe as I first encounter it:

BEST PASTA
By Marcella Hazan. Nominated by Ruth Rogers
Sugo fresco di pomodoro

Ruth Rogers: 'People are always putting yet another ingredient into pasta dishes but for me, and for most Italians, the simplest tomato pasta sauce is always the best. My husband is Italian and that's what he loves the most. When we entertain, which isn't very often, people always expect a fancy meal but I often make this dish because it's the nicest dish there is. The trick is to slow-cook the tomato and if you are using cans of tomato make sure you get rid of the excess juice. This is a fabulous recipe. Enjoy.'

Serves 6

450g pasta
6 tbs extra virgin olive oil
2 medium garlic cloves, peeled and sliced very thinly
300g tinned Italian peeled plum tomatoes, cut into
    large pieces, with their juice
salt
black pepper in a grinder
10 fresh basil leaves, torn by hand into small pieces

Put the oil and garlic in a saucepan and turn the heat to medium. When the garlic becomes coloured a pale gold, add the tomatoes and turn the heat down to very low. Cook, uncovered, until the oil floats free of the tomatoes, for about 20 minutes. Add salt and grindings of pepper and cook for another two to three minutes, stirring from time to time. Off the heat, stir in the torn basil leaves.

Chef's note: The special taste of the sauce depends largely on the way the garlic is handled. It must be sliced very thinly, sautéed only until it becomes just faintly coloured, and then allowed to simmer slowly in the tomato so that it can release all its sweetness. Raw basil at the end contributes a fragrant fillip. Make sure the basil does not undergo any cooking. The sauce can be cooked several hours in advance. Add the basil after reheating, as serving.

The newspaper credits the source text for Rogers's recipe as *Marcella Cucina* by the Italian-born American cook-writer-translator, Marcella Hazan. But when, ten years after finding Ruth Rogers's recipe online, I go looking for the 'original' and finally buy a second-hand copy of the book cited in the newspaper and look through the index hoping to have a special moment with the source, I cannot find the recipe. The recipe is not in the book. I put so much hope in finally reading the original version of the recipe, the recipe that has taught me so much and is still teaching me how to live. The newspaper has listed the wrong book, or perhaps Rogers has forgotten where she first read the recipe, having lived with it for so long that the text has become buried in her archive, no longer read from the page. I give up my search for a while.

Several years after that, in an online search I find a version of the recipe in a scan of another book by Hazan, *Essential Classics of Italian Cooking*, which is a definitive amalgamation of two earlier books. The *Essential* book is quite expensive, as are the two books which were combined to make its contents, now second-hand rarities: *The Classic Italian Cookbook: The Art of Italian Cooking and The Italian Art of Eating* and *The Second Classic Italian Cookbook*. I do not know how the books were combined to make the definitive book – if they were thoroughly mixed together, gently folded in or arranged consecutively. I cannot be sure which book contains the first publication of the recipe by Marcella Hazan, nor do I know if the recipe in the earlier books is the same as in the later *Essential* book. My search for the source of the recipe is not going smoothly, even though Hazan is popular and her books are widely distributed.

In the version of the *Essential Classics* text that I can see online, Hazan gives an introduction that situates the recipe in a historical context.

TOMATO SAUCE WITH GARLIC AND BASIL

This is one of many versions of the sauce Romans call *alla carrettiera*. The *carrettieri* were the drivers of the mule-driven or even hand-pulled carts in which wine and produce were brought down to Rome from its surrounding hills, and the sauces for their pasta were improvised from the least expensive, most abundant ingredients available to them.

Serves 4

1 large bunch fresh basil
900 g/2 lb fresh ripe tomatoes prepared as described [else-where in the book]
or 500 g/1 lb 2oz tinned imported Italian plum tomatoes, drained and cut up
5 cloves garlic, peeled and finely chopped
5 tablespoons extra-virgin olive oil
salt
freshly ground black pepper
450 g/1 lb pasta

NOTE Do not be alarmed by the amount of garlic the recipe requires. Because it simmers in the sauce, it is poached rather than browned, and its flavour is very subdued.

RECOMMENDED PASTA The ideal shape for tomato *alla carrettiera* is thin spaghetti, spaghettini, but ordinary spaghetti would also be satisfactory.

1 Pull all the basil leaves from the stalks, rinse them briefly in cold water and shake off all the moisture using a colander or a salad spinner, or simply by gathering the basil loosely in a dry tea towel and shaking that two or three times. Tear all but the tiniest leaves by hand into small pieces.
2 Put the tomatoes, garlic, olive oil, salt, and several grindings of pepper into a saucepan, and turn the heat to medium-high. Cook for 20–25 minutes or until the oil floats free from the tomato. Taste and correct for salt.
3 Off the heat, as soon as the sauce is done, mix in the torn-up basil, keeping aside a few pieces to add when tossing the pasta.

In her introduction Hazan says she is giving us a version of a Roman dish developed by drivers of carts carrying produce from the hills down into the city. She does not give a date or source for her information, though the handcarts and absence of motorized vehicles give the impression the recipe is generically *old*. However, it seems that the dish emerged for much the same reason that I chose the recipe from the list online – for the cheapness and abundance of the ingredients.

Hazan's recipe is written in English, with the Italian 'alla carrettiera' to refer to her description of its history as a recipe prepared by workers pulling handcarts. Ruth Rogers's version of the recipe is also written in English, though she gives a descriptive title in Italian 'Sugo fresco di pomodoro'. Giving the title in Italian matches the style of her own recipe books named after the River Cafe which is her restaurant (in partnership with Rose Gray before her death). They are both the 'same' recipe, both in English, but they are not the same. Each is a textual annotation of the cook's preferred translation of the recipe at a certain point in time.

Hazan offers suggestions for fresh and tinned tomatoes and Rogers only includes tinned. This is ironic as Rogers's Italian title states that it is 'fresh tomato sauce'. Rogers uses six tablespoons of olive oil, Hazan five; Hazan uses five garlic cloves, Rogers, two; Hazan uses a bunch of basil, Rogers uses *ten leaves.* Hazan begins her instructions by devoting great care to the preparation of the basil, taking all the leaves off the stalks before washing, drying and tearing them into small pieces by hand.

Rogers gives no instructions for washing the basil leaves but emphasizes that they must not undergo any cooking. If the dish is to be reheated and eaten later, the basil must be added at the later time and not when the sauce is first cooked.

Rogers contextualizes the recipe according to its role in her own life. I feel a distant familiarity with Rogers because my mother has the *River Cafe Cookbook* (1996), which is full of recipes based on dishes served at her restaurant. I have encountered Rogers through my mother's translations of her recipes, often for special occasions (pork loin with vinegar, bay leaves and peppercorns is one of my favourites). There is a tradition of *River Cafe Cookbook* 'reception' in my family home. However, neither I nor my mother has eaten at Rogers's restaurant, chiefly because of the expense of its menu. We have not made a pilgrimage to the site of origin; we know her food through my mother's translations.

In her introduction to the recipe on the *Guardian* website Rogers sets up a tension between what people expect her to cook when they come round for dinner and what she cooks. People are surprised when she cooks this recipe with its few, relatively inexpensive ingredients. She says she cooks it 'because it's the nicest dish there is'. When I first find the recipe online, this statement is an exciting invitation to encounter a tin of tomatoes, garlic cloves and olive oil in a new way. Before I follow Rogers's instructions, I do not hold these ingredients in particular regard, but as I enact the recipe's instructions, I become aware of their expansiveness, which suddenly stretches before me. I find myself at the beginning of a hot red epic.

Hazan gives space to the material circumstances that produced the recipe (as far as she knows). She does not claim those conditions as her own, and she does not to deny the living that went into producing the recipe. Yet her refusal to claim total ownership of the recipe does not exclude the possibility of her own authorship, her new translation, her 'again-writing' of the recipe. (Kate Briggs)

Hazan herself writes the recipe 'again' several times: when I receive a grant, I buy more of her books and find three further versions. I decide it is time to take my research into the kitchen and cook the oldest version of the recipe I have found by Hazan, which is subtly different from the one I have cooked a thousand times.

However, my return to the 'origin' of the recipe does not go smoothly. I try to cook the source text for several months but somehow, I can't. I almost cook it. I cook in tangential relation to it. It feels strangely taboo to try. My appetite is in the present tense, and it will not defer to the authority of the original. I turn away. In my search for the source, even though it is conducted with a pinch of salt, I have concerned myself too much with the recipe as a text. I have put too much pressure on myself to embody a bone-dry, unspattered ideal. The recipe becomes stuck in language. I cannot receive it.

I write a diary of my attempts to cook Hazan's original recipe, which becomes a document of refusals and diversions –

A day or two in bed, very tired. Bad television to slow my mind. Bad sleeping. Full pink moon this week.

I have been thinking about making the recipe – the 'living' pot of basil from Morrisons has been sitting on the table for several weeks. But I am also tired and somehow the thought of it does not excite me. In fact more than tired I am melancholic. You mentioned you had bought a can of tuna before you left the room earlier. A fact I forget as I contemplate a piece of smoked bacon. Then I put it back in the fridge and pick up the tin of tuna and think of being in Palermo in Sicily 3.5 years ago when I was alone and in this same melancholy mood. I revisit a recipe for cooking fish with pasta that I wrote then, 'A Spell to Purge Melancholy on Halloween':

remove your bra from beneath your black silk shirt and toss it aside. spin round on the balls of your feet once or enough so you begin to feel like you can move. make your way to the kitchen and open a cold beer and put on a large pan of water to boil with a spoon of salt and dance to music that provokes the melancholy you wish to purge. hearing the music is difficult but the melancholy must be brought to the surface. when the water is boiling hard add in three single handfuls of dried pasta. if tears appear and roll down your cheeks let them fall and take a moment to dance and note how the hot water in the pan is also releasing your melancholy in furious bubbles. in a frying pan melt four anchovies into four tablespoons of olive oil and then add a clove of sliced garlic and half a tablespoon of dried tomato paste to fry gently. stir it so it breaks up. turn off the heat in the anchovy pan after a few minutes and add in a ladle of pasta water and toss the pan to emulsify the oil with the flavourings. when the pasta is a little bit chewy also giving, drain it and toss it in the oil pan with a pancake tossing motion, if the pieces of pasta are not moving enough, add another 2 tablespoons of water and toss again until they move easily in the pan and you can coat them in red oil. eat it with your beer. when your melancholy begins to lessen, put on a song that cheers you and spin round three times. wash up tomorrow.

Back here, now today, hearing music on the radio – Kindness, 'That's Alright' – takes me to a period eight years ago defined by loneliness, yearning and anxiety, but also moments of sudden joy while dancing or cooking. I pick up *Sicilian Food: Recipes from Italy's Abundant Isle* by Mary Taylor Simeti as I did in Palermo when I bought swordfish at the market so I could cook her pasta recipe with diced swordfish, tomato, mint and mozzarella. I do not have swordfish here, but tuna is its kin in texture (I think) and I leaf through MTS's *Sicilian Food* entries on tuna, too; though she has no suggestions for pasta sauce. Taylor Simeti gives a recipe for tuna ragu that includes cinnamon in the sauce (a stick), but she uses a very large whole piece of tuna and I only have a small tin. It is served with boiled potatoes and I want pasta. However, its flavours are shared with the swordfish otherwise – mint, tomato (though it uses concentrate) and garlic. I bring the tuna ragu recipe into dialogue with the swordfish and with Rogers's recipe. I pour a large Campari with one ice cube. I dance and feel my melancholy intensify. I very slowly begin to cook, barely cooking for dancing. I peel two cloves of garlic, spill a lot of olive oil pouring it from a metal container into a bottle with a funnel, already slightly drunk on the alcohol and the music and suddenly everything has oil on it. I pour some of the overflowing oil from the funnel into a pan turn on the heat and add the whole cloves of garlic. The cloves brown slowly flavouring the oil and I think of how my Neapolitan friend in student accommodation introduced me to this method with garlic. Then I see a passage from the *Odyssey* quoted on the page of Taylor Simeti's book in which the cyclops Polyphemus makes cheese and I read it –

A practiced job he made of it, giving each ewe her suckling; thickened his milk, then, into curds and whey, sieved out the curds to drop in withy baskets, and poured the whey to stand in bowls cooling until he drank it for his supper. (trans. Robert Fitzgerald)

You walk in briefly wanting to wash up in here (it is my turn, but I have been fatigued in bed and it is kindness that you are offering; you are worrying I will tire myself out), but I want to be alone in my melancholy that your entry has ruptured and you realize and leave the room. I am not really here, am reinhabiting other moments' acute feelings of euphoria and sadness. I go with it I pour more Campari its luminous redness making this more of a ritual. I add a tin of tomatoes to the oil and garlic cloves I think of her and him in that club and dancing together. So much undone washing up eating breadsticks dipped in spilled oil.

I strip mint leaves from the soft supermarket plant and rinse and roughly chop them and add them to the oil, garlic and tomato. I take half a lengthy cinnamon stick and drop it in after 5 minutes I open the tin of tuna and add it with the oil it is submerged in and stir it and turn the heat down. I put on the song

'Gurbet' by Özdemir Erdoğan and spin round and text D and A. Another of Simeti's tuna recipes had celery in so I boil celery and lemon skin in the salted water for my pasta and dress it as a salad with a little sugar salt oil and lemon juice. I cook pasta and toss it with the sauce but when I begin to eat I scream – a spider has come down from the ceiling and landed on my plate. She walks amongst the spaghetti.

Before when I made the swordfish in Palermo there was a large black fly in my bag of fish. It follows, I suppose, a spider after a fly. The melancholy the spell the music the recipe the mint the fish the ritual of dancing alone in the kitchen, haunted and summoning ghosts with a hot red sauce.

*

I am growing basil from seed for the recipe – I think I have never quite appreciated the importance of basil, but Marcella emphasizes its preparation in her version of the recipe in *The Essentials of Italian Cooking*. I keep thinking about cooking it then deciding not to. Like on Saturday night I was geared up to do it and had imagined its fresh and rich flavour in my mouth and a bitter salad with it. But then I had a fight with you about beetroots. I retreated upstairs and watched a banal American series about a family of witches in small-town white America and you came upstairs and really apologized. You cooked in the end, a tomato sauce with ricotta quite different to the recipe. I sat in the kitchen while you cooked and we talked. You made garlic bread. You used a little, not all of the supermarket basil I bought for the sauce. It has been in the kitchen too long. It is beginning to wilt, and I begin to think I cannot make the recipe with it; it is not adequate for '1 large bunch fresh basil'. I guess I can always buy more but I don't know if I'm ready to return to the sauce. It is too uncannily like looking at myself in the mirror, a task which rarely fails to evoke difficult feelings. Am I growing basil for the sauce or against it? It will be months before the basil I am growing from seed is ready to harvest.

A few weeks later I make the sauce in a way that is more or less Hazan's recipe as it was first published in the UK, but it is a confusing experience and I am distracted and I forget to write down precisely what happened so there is no record. However, it contains unexpected steps, like adding all of the sauce ingredients to the pan at once.

∗

A few months after I document my failed attempts to cook the recipe in my diary, I go to Rome for a few months to do a writing and research residency. Before I leave, I get very excited about the thought of going on a physical pilgrimage. I imagine finding the road where handcart-pullers of

Hazan's recipe worked. I think about going to the market and asking in very limited Italian about sauce alla carrettiera, buying the ingredients – which would be especially fragrant in Rome – and gaining some new insight into the sauce. I think about going to a few different trattorias and ordering pasta alla carrettiera and a glass of red wine and comparing the slightly different methods of cooking the recipe. None of these things take place. I do a lot of work and eat most of my meals in the canteen of the institution where I am staying. I forget about my plans to find the 'origin' of the recipe. The rest of the meals are eaten with a group of people and the restaurants we visit do not serve pasta alla carrettiera. But when I am talking to the residence and estate manager of the institution, she tells me that the retired canteen cook told her that forty or fifty years ago, when there was no money, they served forty grams of pasta with tomato sauce for lunch and dinner every day.

The only meal I cook for myself in Rome is when I forget to sign up to the canteen lunch on a day when lasagne is on the menu. The lasagne is pre-portioned. I have a few supermarket tomatoes in my cupboard in the communal kitchen and a tin of anchovies but no garlic. I have no pasta. But there is a bag of pasta left from previous residents in the kitchen and the new director of the institution, the first woman to lead it, has opened her garden to residents. I pick rosemary and cut it up finely and put it in olive oil with a few anchovies on a low heat. I cut up the almost violently red tomatoes and add them to the pan. The water for the pasta takes a very long time to boil because the diagram for the hobs is incorrect – but I do not know this. While I am waiting for the water to boil and before I have realized there is a problem, I receive a letter that makes me cry. Even though I am frustrated by the slow water, I am glad to have the time to cry. Eventually I realize the problem with the hob and move the pan and the water boils and the pasta cooks and the edges of the tomatoes collapse, and they mix with the oil, the anchovies and the rosemary and just before serving I add a few salty green olives cut into slices as there are some in the fridge. I eat the dish of tomatoes and pasta alone, as I need to.

I was tired from walking on the cobbled streets and from working and it was lunch time but there was no lunch for me in the canteen. There were tomatoes in the cupboard and pasta on the counter and herbs in the garden. I cooked lunch in Rome with what I had to hand, and the source of the recipe reappeared like an echo.

The recipe is a siren-text, an 'I' that also speaks as 'we' and 'they' and 'you'.
It draws us in and makes room.

Unlovely Translations

The word I encounter most often when I tell people I am writing about cookery is *lovely*. It makes me want to tear my hair out. Often, I temporarily lose the power of speech. When people ask about my work an assumption hangs in the air that I am writing a *lovely* book of *lovely* recipes that will be beautifully photographed. That I will use joyful, sensual language about food and eating in idyllic, softly lit settings. That I will be the performer of a perfectly feminine display – a Romantic-era 'lovely maid', perhaps, also erring towards the maternal. When my writing about cooking is described as 'lovely', it is positioned in a benign and pleasant linguistic frame. This is not the fault of whoever utters the word 'lovely'. Much writing about food *is* lovely and comforting, but not all of it must be, and the feeling that it should is a symptom of the culture that underestimates the recipe.

'Lovely' is an acutely gendered adjective that brings my body into the discussion of my writing. It defines my writing through my body which in turn is implicitly defined through an archaic and normative understanding of the word 'woman'. An endless loop that makes everything smaller. The word 'lovely' is applied because the subject matter has been through the same process. Cookery writing is defined through women's bodies which are defined by a massive, crushing apparatus of myth and prejudice and norms. I feel discomfort at being constrained under the sign of 'lovely', located on the side of the so-called virtuous. 'Lovely' is part of the fairy-tale virgin/whore fiction that denies women's humanity, intellect and labour. I think of T.S. Eliot's allusion to 'When lovely woman stoops to folly' in *The Waste Land* (1922). In Eliot's poem the line appears ironically after a woman has boring but also quite violent casual sex. He is quoting *The Vicar of Wakefield*, an eighteenth-century novel popular with Victorian readers, in which it is the first line of a self-condemnatory song written by a young woman after being 'seduced' –

> When lovely woman stoops to folly,
>   And finds too late that men betray
> What charm can sooth her melancholy,
>   What art can wash her guilt away?
>
> The only art her guilt to cover,
>   To hide her shame from every eye,
> To give repentance to her lover,
>   And wring his bosom—is to die.

The other side of loveliness is death! 'Lovely' is used to encourage good behaviour: *lovely woman writes lovely book about cooking*. It suggests that by writing about food I will be obedient. 'Lovely' carries the instruction: do not stray from the lovely path. What is the opposite of lovely? My dictionary gives it as 'ugly', or 'hideous' – the other side of the fairy tale, the path of disobedience and shame and ruin. Do not be ugly or difficult or angry or complex or sensual or anything but blandly lovely. 'Lovely' defines and excludes the non-lovely and works to legitimize violence against those who differ from the ideal of an obedient, quiet, thin, clean, happy, grateful, rich, white woman.

'Lovely' works to conceal the reality of the subject matter; it is an aestheticization that flattens. The proximity of 'lovely' to 'love' is too close to be a coincidence, too. It is almost a slippage. In writing about the recipe, I am writing about a form of knowledge that is often denied the status of knowledge, that is cast instead as a feminine expression of love, as described by Silvia Federici: 'They say it is love. We say it is unwaged labour'. 'Lovely' is suggestive of work that simply radiates out, barely understood as work, and about which there can be no complaint. Work that is self-sacrificing – but apolitical – and for the love of others. When people tell me that what I am writing about is 'lovely', I do not feel 'lovely'; I feel held in a stranglehold that both idealizes and denies my subject.

Cooking the recipe provokes feelings of ambivalence and anxiety as well as joy and pleasure. And as I trace the genealogy of the recipe in its textual translations, from Ruth Rogers to Marcella Hazan's many different printed versions, I think of researching the many translations of Homer's *Odyssey*. I think of the difference in status between the practice of translating the *Odyssey* and the practice of translating the recipe.

As there are many translations of the recipe, there are hundreds and hundreds of translations of the *Odyssey*, which was first written down in Ancient Greek, roughly in 800 BC. And like the recipe, most people have never encountered the so-called 'original' in Ancient Greek, a text which itself is subject to unending debate among classical scholars as to the actual true 100% authentic original 'version'. There are some who are convinced the final few 'books' of the *Odyssey* were written by someone else. Classical scholars cannot definitively agree on the identity, gender or precise provenance of the author who is named 'Homer', or on the question of whether there was only one author of the *Odyssey*. The search continues in certain quarters. Similarly, the original author of the recipe for sauce alla carrettiera cannot be identified.

But unlike the practice of translating the recipe text into a hot red sauce (or, historically, the work of literary translation in general, which is often overlooked in critical culture), translating the *Odyssey* is accorded high status.

Also, unlike the recipe and literature in general, the *Odyssey* is very rarely if ever translated by women, despite the act of *Odyssey* translation stretching back many centuries.

Unlike the recipe, in the UK, US and Germany (the intellectual cultures with which I am most familiar), there is a great deal of academic scholarship, library space, theories, books, funding and conferences concerning that most exclusive practice of *Odyssey* translation, that story of one man voyaging on a ship and taking knowledge from women, witches and hybrid creatures and saving himself and his property through the domination and slaughter of others. One brilliant man's story written by one brilliant man (it is said).

Unlike the recipe, the *Odyssey* has been described on many occasions as a founding text of Western culture.

How else might we make it?

The first English translation of the *Odyssey* was published in c. 1615, and there have been around sixty English translations since, but none published in full by a woman until Emily Wilson's translation in 2017 (to my knowledge). A key differentiating aspect of Wilson's 'reception' of the *Odyssey* is that she translates the women who work in Odysseus's house as 'slaves' instead of 'maids'. 'Slaves' is closer to the Greek text than earlier translations, which generally use the idealized term 'maid'. Wilson's translation draws the reader's attention to the fact that the women's domestic labour is not consensual, not a choice. The use of the word 'maid' to refer to enslaved domestic workers in earlier translations does several things. Unlike 'slave', which describes the legal status of a person in a slave-owning society, the word 'maid' is connivingly ambiguous.

I am reminded of 'lovely' and its use to refer to cooking and recipes when I think of 'maid', for several reasons. First, like 'lovely', 'maid' occupies a position in a binary and misogynistic moral discourse in which women are either virgins or whores who may, according to that logic, be punished if they acknowledge their sexuality. In the translations of the *Odyssey* that precede Wilson's, the moral justification for killing the 'maids' when Odysseus returns home is that they had sex with the men who want to marry Penelope after Odysseus is given up for dead. These men want to take ownership of Odysseus's possessions, which includes the 'maids'. Wilson highlights how earlier translators have used this misogynistic binary to transform the women from 'maids' to 'sluts' in a long Twitter thread from 2018. Here's a bit of it –

> Many translations import misogynistic language when it isn't there in the Greek. In Fagles' best-selling version, 'You sluts – the suitors' whores!' Lombardo: 'Sluts'. Lattimore: 'Creatures'. Fitzgerald: 'Sluts'. Pope's is the best: 'nightly prostitutes to shame'.

Wilson's translation both refuses the softening effect of 'maid' and its opposite. She is able to show how earlier translators insert nineteenth- and twentieth-century moral drama to obscure the fact that the enslaved domestic workers are killed as part of Odysseus's reassertion of control over his property when he finally returns home. When I read Robert Fagles's translation (before Wilson's is published) at the start of my PhD, I experience his linguistic choices as shockingly violent. However, the morality that makes such shaming language possible is familiar: it is on a continuum with 'lovely' and its use to make cooking into idealized cliché.

Second, like 'lovely', 'maid' does something else: it erases the signs of domestic work. 'Maid' characterizes domestic work as a naturalized part of gender that flows instinctively from the bodies of 'maids' as archetypes of femininity. As a word, 'maid' does not necessarily refer to a domestic worker: it could refer to a girl, a young woman, a virgin. It is a word with the pallor of a golden-haired girl in a nine-teenth-century fairy tale about to be taught a moral lesson that curtails her desire and agency. As well as hiding the reality that the young women in the *Odyssey* are enslaved, the semantic ambiguity of 'maid' has an idealizing force which partially conceals that their work, domestic work, *is* work at all. Behind the veil of 'maid' is the often difficult, complex and exhausting fact of domestic work. It appears instead as a kind of 'natural', 'feminine' emanation.

(There is no mention of recipes during the ten or more years I spend studying at university.)

The history of *Odyssey* translation – who gets to do it and the 'truths' that translators disseminate through their work – is a measure of the dominant social forces at any given moment. The misogynist, capitalist and colonial attitudes that have given us so many 'maids' are also those that have excluded the recipe – and much else – from being treated as 'epic', from archives, and from historical narrative. Through studying the ways that 'maid' is used in *Odyssey* translation, I understand how, in one swift motion, language can both conceal the labour and exploitation of domestic work and repress the potential expansiveness of an activity like cooking.

*

I am sharply reminded of my encounters with the word 'lovely' when I read an essay by the poet and translator Sophie Collins, which takes apart the idea of the 'joyful' translator.

Collins begins with a critique of 'the joy of translation', a phrase which she has 'come across again and again' in reference to the work she does. Collins feels alienated by the phrase. Instead of summoning joy, it brings feelings of 'uncertainty' and 'self-consciousness'. Collins turns to an interview with poet and translator Don Mee Choi, who is asked to name 'the greatest joy' of translating Korean to English. Instead of giving an account of joy, Choi responds by detailing her fear of English ('I am terrified of English') and fear of Korean, 'because I have lived outside of South

105

Korea for a long time, I've become a foreigner to Korean as well.' Choi was first forced to migrate from South Korea to Hong Kong to escape a military dictatorship and then came to America alone as a teenager. The question also causes Choi to reflect on the American obsession with joy in contrast with the misery the US causes elsewhere in the world. Collins describes Choi's understanding of joy as 'a conformist trope, a verbal deposit of the imperial mindset so ubiquitous in Anglophone countries as to be used to sell washing-up liquid'.

I do not deny that writing about the recipe or the act of cooking can feel lovely, at times. But to stop at 'lovely' would be an extraordinarily thin reading of cooking, as well as 'a misrecognition of the translator and her role'.
(Collins)

Who does it serve, to describe the recipe and its translator as 'lovely'?

The recipe is the most epic text that does not have reams of scholarship devoted to it. It is epic and yet is at the scale of a hand, a spoon, a nose.

The recipe is an epic with infinite potential translators.

The recipe is an archive of all life that is too hot too red too wet to become a monument; it is an uncanonizable, uncanonizing sea of sauce.

Refusing the Recipe

Some people find their dependence on recipes intensely vexing. They declare their vexation with great gusto. The more I begin to listen the more I hear a misogynistic culture that, while utterly bound to recipes, has developed manifold ways of verbally degrading them.

There is the 'no-recipe recipe book' by *New York Times* editor Sam Sifton, for example:

> The central proposition of *The New York Times Cooking: No-Recipe Recipes* is simple: you do not need a recipe in order to cook.

I note that for each dish for which there is not a recipe, there is a lists of ingredients on one side of the page, and instructions for how to use them on the other. The only difference I can see is that mostly, Sifton does not specify quantities – though he does give guidance on quantities (and sometimes, he gives quantities). The correct ratio of ingredients and ideal presentation is suggested through photographs of dishes, of the kind you find in a recipe book. There are many styles of recipe writing and Sifton has written a recipe book in a style that he likes.

When posturing home cooks on competitive TV shows are asked about their favourite recipes they often reply with a variation of: 'I don't like to use recipes; I just freestyle it; I like to be creative.' On more than a few occasions I have heard people say, 'I hate recipes.' Failing declarations of hate, people express discomfort. For self-declared recipe haters or deniers, the recipe appears as an affront to their autonomy, almost a threat to their freedom. They think they must throw the baby out with the bathwater and say 'no' to recipes. But the recipe is generous: it makes space for our refusal of it, which is also the insistence on our own appetite.

The relationship between the recipe and the cook is not straightforward. Whether a refusal of the recipe is absolute or moderate, there is an undeniable tension of authorship between the recipe text (and perhaps, if known, its author) and the cook. This tension has given rise to a broad repertoire of sentences, words and phrases in common circulation that I can draw from if I want to describe my own refusal of the recipe. These can include verbal asides, disses, addenda, critiques, textual crossings-out, corrections, marginalia and full rewritings.

Here are some of the ways in which I might describe my refusal of the recipe:

I put my own spin on it
I didn't have X so I used Y instead
I didn't bother with that step
I prefer X, so I made a substitution
I wasn't in the mood for it that way, so I did it this way
I was in the mood for X so I added it
I couldn't afford this ingredient, so I used this cheaper one
You can't find this ingredient in shops here, so I use this instead
They prefer X so I adapted the recipe in this way
etc.

However, if we know how to listen, physical forms of resisting the recipe and verbalizations of resentment or disagreement with the text can also be heard as nascent expressions of voice.

I put my own spin on it

I would go so far as to say that every time a recipe text is performed there is a refusal, whether the cook is conscious of it or not. The partial erasure of a recipe through a dis-obedient performance can signal the tentative emergence of the cook's voice. It is often in the impulse to refuse some aspect of a recipe that the cook finds out what they want to say when they are cooking. The recipe text provides a space, a framework which constrains and instructs but also nurtures and releases the voice of the cook. And the tension between a recipe text and the cook does not end in domination. A recipe can usually be set aside if desired. The decision of the cook to respond to a recipe, to cook with it, is also a kind of tribute.

The recipe is a 'writerly' text (Barthes) *that demands the reader become its producer, its translator.*

When I cook the tomato sauce recipe, I read the text and then I translate it into a hot red sauce, into the dish. I labour over my translation. The materials I work with have agency: the garlic, the tomato, the oil, the salt and the basil (if I have it). And so does the space in which the translation takes place: the kitchen, the stove, the heat and the climate, economics, the mood of this-time-now. In between the recipe text and the finished translation, the dish, there is also me.

How will I perform?

If I am only translating a recipe for myself – cooking myself dinner – I could speculate that a standardized version of the recipe might emerge. Each time I make it, it would be for the 'same' reader, appetite, I, me. But my palate – like that of Marcella Hazan and every cook – cannot be relied upon not to change its tastes. And each time I return to the recipe I meet myself again, differently. Performing the recipe reveals an 'I' that cooks in order to speak.

It is just as important and healthy to articulate unpleasant and difficult thoughts as it is to express joy.

Sometimes when I cook my body is heavy and unwilling. In periods of depression or a bad relationship or when panicked about work or money, or just tired and totally uninterested and when I really do not want to cook and every fibre of my being refuses the recipe, but I do it anyway, my performances of the recipe are agonizing or perfunctory going-through-the motions or furious rush jobs. Then, the recipe becomes a set of instructions to keep me from perishing, utility without flavour; it becomes a life raft only.

The unpredictable 'I that cooks', who resists the recipe again and again, generates many new translations. New recipes. Nonetheless, recognizing cooking as work, and as difficult and as something that cannot always be blithely 'lovely' is useful, freeing even. Such recognition allows cooking to come into view; it becomes possible to see what is required of the cook each time she or they or he translates the recipe. As Sophie Collins writes of her ambivalent feelings towards literary translation, 'Increasingly, however, I know this disaffection to be a source of strength and, ultimately, of creativity.' The cook can begin to feel 'the measure of her powers' (M.F.K. Fisher) as a translator of the recipe text.

My refusals of the recipe have taken many forms; here is a rough taxonomy of some I can recall.

poor performance —	stirring the sauce instead of allowing the oil to slowly rise through the tomato
	not cutting the garlic finely enough or cutting it unevenly
lazy performance —	free-pouring the oil instead of counting spoons
anxious performance —	applying too much heat to hurry the recipe
	adding too much salt before tasting
changing instructions —	crushing the garlic instead of slicing it
changing ingredients —	butter instead of olive oil
	rosemary instead of basil

ELABORATION

adding	capers
	chilli flakes
	sugar or vinegar
	anchovy
	eggs
	chorizo
	peppers and onions
	garlic yogurt garnish
	hot chilli butter garnish
	fried aubergine
	sausages
	tuna
missing out ingredients —	leaving out the basil
	using fewer spoons of olive oil
changing the instructions —	turning the heat up and rushing the sauce
	cooking for longer and over-reducing the sauce
misc. —	using the recipe as a basis for / a constituent of a different dish e.g.
	parmigiana di melanzane
	baked squash in tomato sauce
	eggs in purgatory
	shakshuka
	chicken in honey-garlic-sour-tomato-sauce
	lamb patties in sweet, spiced tomato sauce
	tomato cream sauce

112

Sometimes multiple refusals occur in the same performance of the recipe, one building upon another and another. This is a list of the ways I have engaged with the recipe, the attention I have paid to it, how I have manipulated its grammar to find new expression.

My refusals of the recipe are also how I have learnt to play as an adult. The psychoanalyst D.W. Winnicott describes play as the means through which children and adults are able to be creative –

> It is in playing and only in playing that the individual child or adult is able to be creative and to use the whole personality, and it is only in being creative that the individual discovers the self.

Winnicott's conception of play, which enables his therapeutic subject to become creative, is not obedient. On the contrary, playing has to be spontaneous, and not compliant or acquiescent. It also involves 'the manipulation of objects'. Like a child throwing an object, testing it under different conditions, poking it, sitting on it, smashing it, making it an appendage to other things, pulling it apart, using it as a means through which to see the world, and finally dragging it along the ground at the end of the day or even discarding it entirely, the recipe is a thing with which I play. After cooking the recipe several times I cease to be afraid of it and engage in this kind of play. I rearrange its structure, expand and condense it, stick it to other things or build great structures on top of it.

My playful refusal of the recipe is often not consciously intended or premeditated and is shaped by what is to hand – smells, temperatures, other appetites, moods: the things and people that are around me.

There is an erotics to the way I play with the recipe. The push and pull finds the edges of pleasure. Refusing the recipe is also about finding out or expressing *what I like* and *what I don't like* to experience with my body. Because the primary measure of culinary knowledge is whether it brings pleasure to the body, and to what degree, it is inherently erotic. Culinary knowledge has no authority in a text-only format. The various ways in which all people refuse the recipe is how they demand what they want, now again, now again, differently now, now again. Each new translation of the recipe is an imprint of the body and emotions at a particular moment. Each translation of the recipe offers a peep into the erotics of culinary knowledge: kinks of the palate writ large.

Refusal is play.

Play with your food!

In the hot red odyssey, the epic of a thousand and more dishes, my translations often have an audience. When I cook for other people, I am translating the recipe for them too. But, much more than *for* other people, I am usually also translating it *with* them. The appetites, bodies, and moods and desires that are present participate in the translation of the recipe text. We play together. When I think about the collective and fleeting authorship that emerges around the cooking of a dish in a social context, I think of musicians improvising.

I often listen to jazz when I am cooking – Miles Davis, John Coltrane and Mingus are favourites. The way these musicians pass a refrain around the ensemble, each player turning it over and transforming it while remaining in dialogue, makes me think me of cooking with friends. Every person contributes to the performance; the performance depends on who turns up – and in what mood. Theorist and poet Fred Moten describes Miles Davis and his ensemble performing 'So What' together, playing it differently each night –

> 'So What' is reducible neither to its near nonexistent score nor to some imaginarily definitive initial recording nor to any other of the myriad renditions of this improvisation that Miles's ensemble played almost every night

People I cook with tell me how they want to eat, or they don't tell me verbally, but show me. Or sometimes everyone cuts up ingredients, or stirs the pot, or adds extra seasonings to the dish, or puts unexpected condiments on the table. Everyone changes the recipe. And, given the complexity of the performances it gives rise to, and their infinite variations, the recipe is also a 'near nonexistent score'. However, like the refrains that are the basis of the ensemble's improvisation in all the performances of 'So What', the recipe holds the group together.

Members of the ensemble vary the order in which aspects of the dish are eaten and the way they are cut up, or not. The things that are not eaten. The speed at which eating takes place, fast or slow, and its impact on the temperature of the food. The music that is playing while the eating performance takes place and how music encourages people to eat in time with its rhythm or to talk loudly while eating. Pieces of food that are shared with someone else, and how. The parts of a plate that each person lingers over. Alternatively, there is total refusal and eating none of it, silence, a 'tacet' performance.

There is no best, no most accomplished, no definitive translation of the recipe. No 'imaginarily definitive initial recording'. (Moten) But the act of repeating and changing the refrain together, like the act of cooking the recipe, is also an acknowledgement of our responsibility to the ensemble, historically as well as in the present.

*

Collective refusal to eat bad food can instigate a revolutionary moment, too. In Sergei Eisenstein's film *Battleship Potemkin* (1925), a portrayal of the 1905 uprising off the coast of Odessa, revolution is sparked by sailors in the Tsar's Black Sea fleet refusing to eat borscht made from rotting, maggot-filled meat. The soup reveals the disparity of class positions on the ship: the ship's doctor decides it is acceptable for the sailors to eat the borscht despite graphic footage of the maggots. High-ranking officers threaten to string the sailors up on the yardarm for refusing the soup. But the collective refusal to eat the borscht unites the sailors and in the face of violent threats, their revolutionary discourse turns into a revolutionary moment, and they mutiny, take command of the ship and raise a red flag. Their leader Vakulinchuk, who at the beginning of the film urges the sailors to join with revolutionary forces in Russia, is shot dead by one of the high-ranking officers. His body is brought ashore in Odessa by his comrades with the sign on his chest, 'For a spoonful of borscht', '*Изъ-за ложки борща*', the sight of which moves people on land to support the uprising.

To insist that a person eats food they cannot bear to eat or in circumstances in which they do not want to eat can be as violent as taking it away. To eat is a condition of life, but it is equally necessary to say 'I would prefer not to' eat that, and to insist on one's own difficult body. (Herman Melville) One's own difficult body, through which all pain and pleasure is transmitted, is one's own very alive-ness. When people refuse to eat something or refuse to eat it in the way it is served, they are also demanding that pleasure and nourishment come in the form in which they need it. Refusing the recipe as a cook and at the table also expresses yearning to participate in world-making. A refusal to eat what one is given is also a demand for 'access to the magic of the signifier, to the pleasure of writing' the recipe. (Barthes, trans. Richard Miller)

Consider the Sausage!

Sometimes (always) heroes let you down, which is to say, after reading D. W. Winnicott's illuminating writing on play, I am *shocked and appalled* to find he is among the people who are fond of declaring 'I hate recipes!' *Shocked and appalled* to find his disaffection to be such that he chooses to make cooking from recipes the antithesis of living a playful, creative life. This is not a Good Enough analysis for me. I am compelled to engage with Winnicott on the matter.

In the paper 'Living Creatively', published in 1970, Winnicott describes cooking from a recipe as the antithesis of creativity. Like theorists before and after him Winnicott alights upon cookery as an ideal tool to develop a theory about something else. He takes for granted that a hypothetical recipe-follower (she) may be invoked for his theorizing purposes with no contradiction –

> We can look at the generality or at the details of which creative living is composed... I know that

one way of cooking sausages is to look up the exact directions in Mrs Beeton... and another way is to take some sausages and somehow to cook sausages for the first time ever. The result may be the same on any one occasion, but it is more pleasant to live with the creative cook, even if sometimes there is a disaster or the taste is funny and one suspects the worst. The thing I am trying to say is that *for the cook* the two experiences are different: the slavish one who complies gets nothing from the experience except an increase in the feeling of dependence on authority, while the original one feels more real, and surprises herself (or himself) by what turns up in the mind in the course of the act of cooking. When we are surprised at ourselves, we are being creative, and when we find we can trust our own unexpected originality. We shall not mind if those who consume the sausages fail to notice the surprising thing that was in the cooking of them, or if they do not show gustatory appreciation.

Winnicott finds cooking from a recipe to be an ideal tool for theorizing because it is cooking from a recipe *in theory*. However, a recipe demands translation into praxis and hangs limp if left languishing in theory only. In his theorizing, Mrs Beeton, the recipe, the sausages, the cook and the sausage-eaters are all very well behaved and do his bidding with no complications. He is able to define his generic model of 'creative living' by constructing a neat binary: there is the person who cooks sausages using a recipe, and the person who cooks sausages without using a recipe. There is 'the slavish one who complies' (phrasing suggestive of the colonial-misogynistic discourse in which Winnicott has marinated), 'while the original one feels more real'. The ordering of these binary statements – 'slavish' then 'original' – is mirrored by the ordering of gender as Winnicott names the cook: 'herself (or himself)'. The possibility of a male cook is consigned to parenthesis; really, he is in a different room.

Where is the spattering?

I wonder: where is the account of cooking given by the recipe follower *herself*? Winnicott does not appear to write from the details of his own experience of cooking. The 'strict discipline' to which he holds himself in his psychoanalytic practice, where he 'withholds interpretations' of a patient before the patient arrives at the interpretation themselves, has lapsed. The generosity he accords his analysands, whose lives form the basis of his theorizing, is missing too. In fact, there is no patient who cooks and therefore nothing to analyse except his own thoughts about cooking projected onto an abstract cook. In the case of this imagined recipe-follower, Winnicott is happy to cast aspersions. He does not allow the cook to become more than abstract: he is happy to silence her so that he can make his argument.

Winnicott also sets aside the hungry bodies for whom the 'creative cook' cooks when he says, 'it is more pleasant to live with the creative cook, even if sometimes there is a disaster or the taste is funny and one suspects the worst'. It is fanciful and alien to the mind of a cook responsible for feeding people with any kind of regularity to dismiss the importance of food being edible. If food is not edible there might be a jovial response; there could also be anger or anxiety or stomach pain at night from hunger. And if those eating give no response at all to delicious and surprising food then apparently, the cook will feel nothing about it – 'We shall not mind if those who consume the sausages fail to notice the surprising thing that was in the cooking of them, or if they do not show gustatory appreciation.' Who are the people sitting at Winnicott's table with no appetites and no emotions? In Winnicott's theory I cannot find evidence of the cook, the recipe, the sausages or those who eat, only his unscorched hands, clean shirt and a method for knowledge production about what it means to cook that has been engineered outside of the kitchen.

As there is no identifiable case study in Winnicott's theory, only the straw men of 'the slavish one' and the 'the original one', I make myself the patient. I experiment on myself to test Winnicott's theory of creative living. I find the recipe for frying sausages in *Mrs Beeton's Book of Household Management* to see if I get 'nothing from the experience except an increase in the feeling of dependence on authority', as Winnicott prophesies. I go shopping to buy sausages after a morning of work, and then I make them for lunch. As I cook, I scrawl down a few small details on the back of an envelope so that I don't forget them. After eating, I leave the kitchen and write an account of following the recipe by hand in a notebook. That text is transcribed here (I write in a large scrawl, and it is a small notebook, hence the short lines.) –

I made Mrs Beeton's
recipe for frying sausages
for ~~it~~ the first time.
I found the recipe on
Google Books, it is a
19th century version, I
am not sure which
edition. I looked to
the sausages to relieve
me from a feeling of
abstraction that arose from
tying myself in knots
writing. It is like a
mist descends, I felt
distant from the world,
bodies, things. I went
especially to buy the
sausages at a nearby
butcher. I am not a
particular fan of the
butcher – I have had
strange experiences there
in the past. But one
of their sausages is

quite nice. I bought
12 sausages, 6 for today
6 for another time.
At home I washed the
pan I felt would be
the best host for the
sausages. Mrs Beeton does
not specify, apart from
'a frying-pan'. I chose
a pan not too snug,
as I did not want them
to semi-steam and not
so large that they
would scorch + lose their
moisture. Cast iron.
I put the radio on, it is
1980s day on the radio
station when I turn it
on, lots to dance to,
the soaring desire-anguish-
filled male falsetto voice
of the 80s and rap
and pop with samples.
I take the sausages
out of the bag and
separate them with a
small knife. They are
gorgeously fat and I can
see flecks of pepper
and herbs.

I turn the I try to
prick them with a fork
as Mrs Beeton
instructs but the tines
are too blunt to penetrate
the sk casing so I use
the end of a small
knife with a black handle (from IKEA)
I turn the oven on
and put in two plates
to warm (I do not
want it all to become
cold.) I cut a 1 inch
by 0.5 cm piece of
butter (lightly salted)
and put it in the
pan and watch it
melt. I was unsure
whether to do this.
Mrs Beeton writes
'put them into a frying-
pan with a small piece
of butter'. Perhaps half-
following another recipe
I decided to melt the
butter first. It was
barely a decision.
I added the sausages.
It was a low-medium heat
(though Mrs Beeton does

not specify a heat).
I set a timer for 12 minutes   (Mrs Beeton specifies
10–12 minutes)
The music keeps
interrupting my attention.
Perhaps it is my return to
things, flesh, the world.
I can't stop dancing.
Chaka Khan 'I feel
for you' comes on,
and after a period
of feeling out-of-
my-body (the winter,
lockdown, fatigue, anxiety)
like a surge of sap
rising I am
electrified full of
desire and movement
dancing dancing dancing I
        am horny
exuberant hot I make
coffee. Hot sausages
and hot coffee and
hot toast. I grind
some beans with the
hand grinder, dancing
all the while. I
fill the kettle with water
and press the switch.
I turn the sausages

seeing that they have
bronzed browned on the
side that was in the
hot butter. As Mrs
Beeton instructs I turn
them a few more times
though I do not quite
keep the pan moving as
she instructs.
It is my first time
cooking the recipe; I
am very excited. It is
bringing me to life. I do
not think I have noticed
sausages bronzing caramelizing
in this way before.
I pour hot water
over ground coffee.
I tighten my apron
to feel the strings
tighter over my body as
I dance, flying on some
kind of libidinal high.
I think of Winnicott's
dry sausage-less account
of following this recipe.
I cannot have quite
pricked the sausages
enough with the knife —
several have split slightly,

one is coming perversely
out of its casing at
one end.
They did not explode
though, as they might
have, had I not
pricked them. I thought
of his account of cooking
sausages without a
recipe as if 'for
the first time'. But
(she) he could only cook the
sausages at all because
other recipes were
floating in the air because
an imagination of a
recipe is present.
When I cook this recipe
it is as if I approach
sausages for the first
time.
I find my fat
sausages need more
time than Mrs Beeton
allows. There are parts
that remain pink
even after 12 minutes
have elapsed and I had
turned them as she
said. I begin to feel

127

concern about dryness
or over and under cooking.
While I finish them,
I cook the toast and
butter it and put it
on the plates in the
oven. Mrs Beeton does
not mention butter but
not using it seems
too dry. Finally,
I put two sausages
on each plate with   (& two more in the pan for seconds)
toast. On the table are
french and english
mustards, ketchup and
brown sauce. I only
use the mustards.
The sausages are
exquisitely juicy.
                    I love it.
            After we have eaten
            the Cure 'pictures of
you' is on the radio.
While I write up
I am sending messages
to D + A and
among other things
we discuss the
dramatic imprecision of
predicting when a

baby will be born.
One of them (A)
was due over a week
ago.
'it's just amazing
how imprecise it actually
is in terms of estimated
due date and how very
very different each
mother-baby pair is'

Over lunch I say
that I like that
Mrs Beeton gives an
average cost
and a season for
sausages, and a
note about hot weather
and a historical footnote
about Saxon Swineherds!!

Wow-ee!

After I cook the sausages, I am more in disagreement with
Winnicott than before. His account of cooking from the
recipe reduces the experience to a thin linguistic apparition.
Cooking *does not take place in the medium of language.*
In his haste to theorize, Winnicott mistakes the recipe text
on the printed page for the act of cooking the recipe. Mrs
Beeton's recipe text is a series of steps with explanatory

points, as if to cook were to progress from point A to B
on a two-dimensional line –

FRIED SAUSAGES

838. INGREDIENTS. — Sausages; a small piece of butter.

Mode. — Prick the sausages with a fork (this prevents them
from bursting), and put them into a frying-pan with a small
piece of butter. Keep moving the pan about, and turn the
sausages 3 or 4 times. In from 10 to 12 minutes they will
be sufficiently cooked, unless they are *very large*, when a
little more time should be allowed for them. Dish them with
or without a piece of toast under them and serve very hot.

[An extract of the instructions, not including the illustration or the note about Saxon swineherds, nor
the note on how warm weather affects sausages pre-refrigeration, nor the average cost and season.]

Mrs Beeton's austere imperatives constrain the explosive
potential wreckage of cooking, of bodies that cook. They
offer support. The minimalism of the recipe text is in a
dialectical relationship with the total possible edible world
and everything I might do with my body. Cooking takes
place in at least three dimensions. An intense and whirling
experience of time emerges as I cook, it's a wild ride. It is
the beginning of spring after a winter trapped inside and
I am in need of release. My experience of cooking Mrs
Beeton's sausages is that of time as change, not the clock-
time minutes on a timer. But her recipe makes cooking
the sausages navigable and not spiralling, formless chaos,
despite my mood. The text assembles the elements, suggests movements and sets the essential boundaries through
which form can emerge.

And what form!

There are no fizzing, grease-spitting, *spattering* sausages in Winnicott's account of cooking the recipe, and no impatient appetite. Where is his hand his nose his tongue his salivating the grease on his shirt? The pale flaccid flop of a British-type sausage before it is cooked? Winnicott's account of the recipe removes the sausages from the recipe for sausages. And also, removes the cook from cookery. Winnicott sucks the life from the recipe and the recipe-follower (*her*), consuming them as raw material for his theorizing about what it is to live 'creatively'. But despite his vampirism, Winnicott's account is missing all the blood – yours, his, mine, the sausage's, the pig's, the farm labourer's, the blood of those seated at the table, or on the sofa, or not seated at all.

✻

Winnicott fears the mothering hand of the recipe on the sausage (on his sausage). He, a psychoanalyst, chooses a sausage to make his argument – the most phallic of all foodstuffs – and Mrs Beeton, who is THE MOTHER OF ALL RECIPE WRITERS. In a rather small voice he says,

'Hands off my sausage, Mrs Beeton!'

Winnicott's fear of creative castration by the mother-of-all-recipe-writers provokes a childish rejection of recipes as a form. He exaggerates the authority of the recipe because he fears what it signifies, thinking to himself,

'I, Winnicott, cannot be taught by you, Mrs Beeton!'

Winnicott denies the recipe as a method for producing insights into its subjects: the sausages and the cook. In fact, he positions the recipe as the opposite of a method for discovery. In his narrative, the recipe is more closely aligned with a path to *unknowing* that which it concerns. Winnicott denies the recipe-writer is a producer of knowledge, too. Winnicott denies Mrs Beeton – who went into labour with a child aged twenty-eight while reading the proofs for the recipe book containing her method for frying sausages, and then died! Her labour of research through cooking practice and/or reading and/or conversation is for naught in Winnicott's analysis. Her work should be set to one side. He makes it invisible. The recipe should be set to one side. The recipe is a threat to the creative flourishing of 'the original one'. Winnicott can only see the recipe as negative limitation on (his) powers of creativity. He includes himself in a collective 'we' only when elaborating on how cooking without a recipe liberates creativity within the subject. His conceptualization of originality is a fantasy of genius unconnected to other knowledge, emerging miraculously from an un-dependent subject, at the beginning of time, with unmediated access to the world...

As Jacqueline Rose writes in an essay on mothers (and the hatred of mothers) –

As if genuine neediness – being, or having once been, a baby, is what this Conservative rhetoric most hates... The one who most loudly proclaims the ideal of iron-clad self-sufficiency must surely have the echo of the baby in the nursery hovering in the back of his or her – mostly his – head. (Jacqueline Rose)

Using the powers he has cultivated professionally (psycho-analytic theorizing) Winnicott tries to destroy the recipe and her attendant labourers (the cook and the recipe writer) and any power they might have over him. He does not see that they hold him anyway, have already accommodated him and held him and allowed him to throw them on the floor, to pretend he does not live in a reality made by the recipe for sausages, and to dream of his omnipotence over sausages. Winnicott does not wish to know that the recipe and the sausage have always coexisted. There has always been a sausage recipe with which he would inevitably collaborate, and which he would inevitably repeat, despite his desire for unmediated contact with the sausages, despite his desire to become 'the original one'. Winnicott wishes to encounter and mould the sausages as if he were a superman or child-god, and not contingent on, or entangled with, the labour and the ideas of others. He does not want to know that his mother has already saved him a hundred times. And the sausage-makers and the recipe writers and farm workers, the sun, the water, the earth.

'No man is an island entire of itself' (John Donne)

Winnicott misses the insight that the recipe can restore the body to language when they are adrift from one another, and that this return will be different each time it is repeated. The sausage returns to the word when I cook Mrs Beeton's recipe. The sausage is no longer an apparition, not the bloodless ghost sausage of Winnicott's theory, and I am no longer a tangle of words only. Mrs Beeton gives me an approach to cooking and eating sausages that I at turns follow and refuse, and through which I am able to return to myself after a difficult period of drifting through language. Enacting her method jolts me back into my body.

When I cook from Mrs Beeton's recipe my body speaks and wants again after months in hibernation: it is a spring awakening. I cannot deny the libidinal force of the sausages on a Thursday afternoon in April. A composition with toast and two mustards. Dancing and desire, thinking about fucking every which way. And I could do it again tomorrow and it would be different, and the day after that it would be different again. I move as I have not done for months during the coldest spring in recent memory. The snow melts. As I watch the pale skin turning bronze in the pan and negotiate Mrs Beeton's instructions, all knowing coalesces in the recipe performance, which becomes a new translation, an 'again-writing', (Briggs) though not a writing-over.

The recipe is not something I can simply comply with.

My performance, the sausages, the pan, the dancing, the splitting skins, the apron strings and horniness are not the text, but they are birthed by its nourishing constraint, an embrace. Winnicott says when we cook without a recipe, we open ourselves to surprise: 'When we are surprised at ourselves, we are being creative, and when we find we can

134

trust our own unexpected originality.' When I cook Mrs Beeton's recipe I am surprised, my body is surprised, the sausages surprise me. The recipe gives rise to 'unexpected originality' that is also, as it ever is, *of the world*. The model of creativity that Winnicott produces in response to Mrs Beeton is not of the world, not created in an atmosphere where sausage recipes already circulate like oxygen. There was a recipe for cooking sausages in the air when Homer wrote the *Odyssey* almost 3000 years ago. Winnicott tries to cook up a theory with recipes, but his reverence for an isolated genius comes out in the cooking and shapes an unappetizing dish. Even when I cook without looking at a recipe on a page, I am always referring to an index of recipes in which I, we, are always immersed. Any 'new' dish I make is a composite of fragments I have seen, eaten, heard about in passing and which I repeat in a new constellation, a chimera.

There are recipes of such baroque complexity that to 'comply' feels essential if the dish is to ever be arrived at. Long and complex recipes require a great deal of time and focus if they are not to become oppressively stressful. Though even then, one may still be 'surprised' at what is discovered in the qualities of things revealed in the smaller processes of which a complex recipe is composed. Winnicott does not extend to the sausage, or the butter, or the mind-body of a cook the generous patience he extends to his analysands – to wait for them to unfurl and to find their question, to play and, in playing, to encounter themselves. He does not regard the recipe as a method for enlightenment.

Mrs Beeton's recipe holds me and enables me to play. The sudden compulsion to tighten my apron strings is so that I can feel my body more keenly. I submit to the recipe and am riveted to myself. Presence returns through an encounter with the tightened strings which bring me *back here now*. This too is the function of the recipe, which, like apron strings, is the paradox of a constraint that liberates. As both my performance and the materials with which I cook strain against and pluck at the taut strings of the recipe it produces a music. There is pleasure in restraint, which is to play with and across boundaries. The recipe allows the complex reality of the thing-which-is-not-me to emerge through specific forms of touch. These are not the chilly boundaries of theory-without-bodies, but the kind that fizz hot steam. My fantasy is not of the unfettered mind without a body.

> *Tie me up Mrs Beeton*
> *Yes, tie me up Mrs Beeton!*
>
> (after Katherine Angel)

I could not have known the sausages or myself so intimately in that moment without you, thank you, Mrs Beeton. I need all the available resources to understand what it is to cook the sausages with Mrs Beeton's recipe. As well as the account in my journal, I use the 'draw' function in my Word document to make a diagram of the relationships involved in my cooking the sausages. The more I try to think about it, the more the diagram expands and expands, and I have to stop because I cannot stop expanding it and there is not enough space on the page.

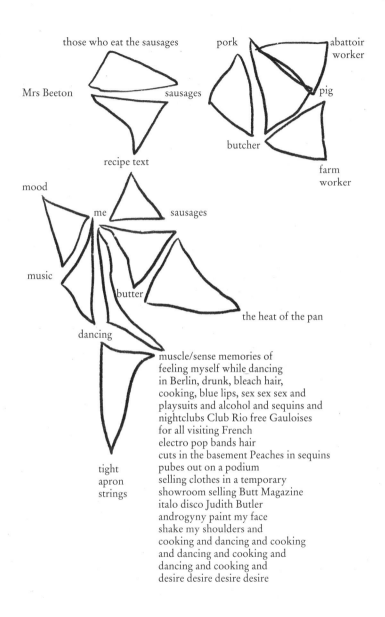

those who eat the sausages

pork

abattoir
worker

Mrs Beeton

sausages

pig

butcher

recipe text

farm
worker

mood

me

sausages

music

butter

dancing

the heat of the pan

muscle/sense memories of
feeling myself while dancing
in Berlin, drunk, bleach hair,
cooking, blue lips, sex sex sex and
playsuits and alcohol and sequins and
nightclubs Club Rio free Gauloises
for all visiting French
electro pop bands hair
cuts in the basement Peaches in sequins
pubes out on a podium
selling clothes in a temporary
showroom selling Butt Magazine
italo disco Judith Butler
androgyny paint my face
shake my shoulders and
cooking and dancing and cooking
and dancing and cooking and
dancing and cooking and
desire desire desire desire

tight
apron
strings

137

To follow a recipe is to enter into the chaos of intersubjectivity, of relation. Me and the sausages and Mrs Beeton, others. When I cook, as when I meet a new person, there is the danger of obliteration, of a loss of self. My performance of Mrs Beeton's score is also a date. A push-pull encounter. The shimmer of a boundary ripe for touch, for crossing over. Butter melted, frothing, not burning. Hot enough for bronzing the pallid skin of the sausages, expelling their moisture, drawing the skin taut: how taut? Too taut, an eruption of steam from within splits one or two.

In Winnicott's example, the recipe is a form of oppression which insists that he conform to the detriment of his creative self. I want to say: *Mrs Beeton is not trying to cook for you.* She is not there. Winnicott projects a scolding mother, but she is not there to force his hand. Winnicott must summon a self, a body to venture towards the other and cook the recipe, and that is what is scary.

Mrs Beeton writes in anticipation of her absence.

Winnicott is simultaneously afraid of speaking and of being silenced. He does not realize that working with the recipe does not exclude the possibility of his voice. He does not see that Mrs Beeton's voice and his own will cohabit and coexist as he cooks. There need be no murder of Winnicott by Mrs Beeton. The recipe Mrs Beeton gives is a facilitation of his voice that is also an echo of hers. There is no language outside or 'before' the recipe available to you, Winnicott. The recipe is an invitation to participate in producing a siren-song. The *inexpressible* richness of embodiment *is contained inexpressibly* within the recipe (Wittgenstein, via Maggie Nelson): it asks that you find this out, begin to speak, to cook.

✳

When I worked in a fish and chip shop aged fifteen, a woman in her late twenties who worked there too told me that the saveloy sausages we served were full of 'ass and ears and eyeballs'. After she had said that, the brick-red tubes sitting hot under the heat lamps, smelling really quite appetizing in the way of highly seasoned meat, became a chant of 'ass and ears and eyeballs'. If you bent them, they would snap and they squeaked slightly when they rubbed against each other. My colleague liked to talk about sex and the body in a matter-of-fact way. I think she told me about the sausages partly because she delighted in saying 'ass and ears and eyeballs'. I liked to hear the words, but I was also embarrassed by her making them known, bringing the hidden ass into view. She was not hiding from the meaning of saveloys when she called out their recipe as she turned battered fish in hot fat.

Sausages are filled with parts of an animal that are not for display. Not loin or chop. Their thin translucent skin contains indistinct minced oddments in a smooth, visually repeated form. Winnicott's theory of creative living mimics the form of the sausage. The sweepings of his unconscious are concealed behind his smooth conclusions, but I glean:

his denial of knowledge produced by feminized labour; anger at his mother, or Mrs Beeton, or all women; fear of his dependence on the labour of others; the allure of unmediated power.

I am calling out the ass and ears and eyeballs!

Homer was more aware of the ass and ears and eyeballs of cooking sausages than Winnicott, too. Homer – he/she/they, and Emily Wilson, write a rich metaphor for Odysseus's fraught emotions in which Odysseus *is a sausage* being roasted by another man –

> So his heart held firm
> and constant, but he writhed around, as when
> a man rotates a sausage full of fat
> and blood; the huge fire blazes, and he longs
> to have the roasting finished. So he squirmed,
> this way and that, and wondered how he could
> attack the shameless suitors, being one
> against a multitude

Homer and Emily Wilson do what Winnicott cannot and make the sausage present on the page with this deeply erotic image of cooking sausages to a commonly understood method, or recipe. They bring its visceral 'squirming' physicality into view. Homer uses the sausage recipe as a metaphor that taps into Odysseus's possessive and sexually jealous rage. He has just seen the enslaved serving girls enjoying time away from their work, 'giggling, happy to be out together'. The girls' joy, his suspicion they have had sex with men he deems inappropriate, and perhaps the fact they are not working, instantly leads Odysseus to thoughts of murder: 'His heart was roused to rage; he wondered whether to jump at them and slaughter every one.' Homer's sausage metaphor shows Odysseus's anger to be erotically charged and violent, full of the blood and writhing and hot spattering I experience when I cook the recipe.

Again and Again,
There is That You

Blushing, I write down what she said –

'I know you want to please me, you've cooked for me.'

I gasp at the thought of being caught in her gaze.

*

Is it too strange to compare cooking to a poem by Rainer Maria Rilke? When I think about cooking for people, I think of 'Archaic Torso of Apollo'. The poem invites me again and again to consider a transformational encounter between self and other, me and *You*. It gets to a feeling I have about being a cook, and my relationship with a person I will cook for. Of beholding, of being unexpectedly beheld, of intimacy and difficulty. The mystery and revelation of the other, and of becoming an other, too. In the poem, a reversal of the subject-object relationship takes place. I recognize this reversal from cooking for the people I meet. It is through this switch of perspective that I have acquired knowledge about the world that is not-me.

The 'Archaic Torso of Apollo', or 'Archaïscher Torso Apollos' as I first read it as a German undergraduate, is a very hot poem. The heat has several sources. There is the thought of being gazed at, as the poet describes the Torso with more than a hint of lascivious intent, the body illuminated by a desiring eye. There is also the heat of resistance as the Torso seizes the subject position and speaks back to the poet, of *I am also looking at you, noticing your strangeness, your vulnerability.* A switch.

It is a short poem but there is a lot going on. The voice of the poem, its 'I', encounters a sculpture of Apollo and speculates about its head, which is missing. She or they or he imagines eyes that ripen like apples. Even the absent parts of the sculpture of Apollo become richly virile and sharp and juicy in the viewer's mind, whose looking is generative of fantasy images, of language, of the poem. The gaze moves down the torso with growing eroticism as it meditates on the curve of loins and its euphemistic 'centre'. Shoulders 'glisten just like wild beasts' fur' and finally the statue bursts forth from its stony confines like a star, like a sun. Then suddenly, in a twist I can never forget, the direction of the gaze is reversed in the poem, and the statue looks at the poet –

denn da is keine Stelle,
die dich nicht sieht. Du mußt dein Leben ändern.

for here there is no place
that does not see you. You must change your life.

(Rainer Maria Rilke, trans. Edward Snow)

The statue looks back and says, 'You must change your life.' The reversal is a surprise, devastating at first. It throws me off balance. The statue speaks. The object speaks. Its speech unsettles a hierarchy produced by grammar, of subject (active) and object (passive). The encounter between the poet and that which he gazes at is revealed to be mutual: the statue is not, was never, silent, and is not an object. The poet is not, is never, a subject alone, and is also the object of another gaze: the poet is also an Other. When the Torso looks back and speaks it suspends the physics of subject-object relations produced by grammar. The doer and the done-to. The Torso cannot be entirely known or contained by the poet's language. The more Rilke's poet tries to describe the Torso, the more he becomes entangled in an intersubjective relationship. The poet is part of the world, not apart from it.

One of the most shocking aspects of the statue looking back and speaking is the revelation that it has secrets, knows things that the poet does not. The poet is the Other to the statue, its not-I, a small gazed-at thing: visible and in relation. The poet must accept that he occupies a limited position. In fact, must accept that he *has* a position and that he can only know so much because of that position.

The poet must give up the attempt at invulnerable transcendence, floating above all he surveys.

I cannot help but see things in terms of dynamics, directions and structures. The cook looking at the person for whom they will cook, describing them through a dish, the I and the You, self and other, subject and object and the difficulty therein. When I set out to cook for someone new, I experience the electrifying reversal of the poem. When I first begin cooking, I have the impulse to make my own ideal dish – the product of my own creative interests – and present it to them for their appreciation. Sometimes I attempt a transcendence which forgets that the eater has agency too, that they have a particular history and palate. I forget they have the power of refusal. They eat in the way that *they* want to. They teach me about the limitation of my own position and of theirs: our mutual specificity. They teach me about difference. The people for whom I cook tell me things I do not know and sometimes, things I do not want to know.

Culinary knowledge is a reaching towards the other, an acknowledgement that our relationship with that which lies beyond us is what will nourish us.

*

I move house fifteen times in twelve years and cover all points of the compass in London. South, then east then south, then west, then south-west then north then east

145

and further east and further east then south and south and south-east. In a contemporary Odyssey most people are blown from place to place not by the wrath of the gods, but by landlords. Landlords can sell the place you are living in even if you have only just moved in, or raise the rent above what you can pay. Landlords are rarely met in person by those whose lives they impact so profoundly. Tenants may experience mouldy walls, poor ventilation, cockroaches, rats, mice, minuscule rooms and deposit theft. A landlord may never set foot in a home they own, which for them is not a place to live.

Almost every time I move house there is a new *You* to get to know.

Cooking compels me to write beyond heteronormative categories of love and desire – there is an erotics and a difficult intimacy to every meal with every *You*.

＊

You are coming and I will go and buy milk. Rice pudding is a comfort to you. Later I can admit it is a comfort to me too. I or we first alight on rice pudding during the 2010 football world cup. In the yellow kitchen with a chequerboard floor I find the recipe in a book and see that there is nothing in it that cannot give you pleasure.

When we meet, I immediately realize I want to give you pleasure. I spend time in the yellow kitchen trying to understand how to cook for you. Cooking will be the way that I give you pleasure. I think of my endeavour as heroic somehow. I want to answer every question and to always save you by cooking you exactly the thing you want most. In contrast, I try to remain unseen and invulnerable behind a display of dramatic clothing and haircuts. As when Odysseus returns home in disguise, it is *as if* I can be seen, when in fact I have put great effort into constructing spectacles that hide my body and emotions.

But in the yellow kitchen I hear the final line from Rilke's poem, 'Du mußt dein Leben ändern', you must change your life. I look at you and consider what I will cook for you, but I find my gaze is wanting. I think of Roland Barthes's reflection on the limits of looking as a means of knowing the other in *A Lover's Discourse* –

> I catch myself carefully scrutinizing the loved body. To *scrutinize* means *to search*: I am searching the other's body... I was looking at everything in the other's face, the other's body, coldly... I was fascinated—fascination being, after all, only the extreme of detachment. (Barthes, trans. Richard Howard)

My scrutiny is not enough to know what to cook for you – I find that instead of looking, I must listen. Detached fascination is not an effective way to find out your pleasures. You are not there to be searched by my eye. Trying to cook for you dispels the illusion that I can be a subject who can look from a distance and see and know things through naming them, and then act. For example: some of the things I think are good to eat make you uncomfortable.

Horror!

The horror of rejection. Sometimes when I cook for you it is as if I am speaking to you, but my words do not land, or even cause pain. I listen again, become the Other and you, the subject. I become an object-subject acted upon and acting through your hunger. (To be clear, you do not ask me to cook for you, but at the time, cooking is what I can do to communicate.) Again and again, I experience the reversal of the last line in Rilke's poem. When I try to cook for you, it becomes clear that I am set in stone, not you. You are the subject whose appetite compels me to change the recipe. We find a way to cook together.

> *I will cook with a Siren voice,*
> *which is I-as-You, as they, as we, as me and you both*

The question of what to cook for you cannot be answered by me alone, it cannot be uncovered by my speculation, and it cannot be my own theoretical concoction. When I cook for you, I cannot turn you into my object. I have to draw close to find out what recipe might sit well on your tongue. The closer I come, the less you are an object. It is not empathy I need, because as I draw close, I find out that I cannot know you fully and that I cannot have your feelings.

Empathy always has a politics; it is about power. I cannot attribute my appetite to you, me eating is plainly not you eating. Cooking makes clear the limitations of empathy: I cannot fantasize your appetite as my own and I cannot eat for you. I can cook what you say you want to eat or accept that you cannot eat what I have presented. The closer I am to you, the more imperceptible you become, and that is OK. Despite my efforts to hide, you see me and don't ask me to leave. You let me cook for you in the yellow kitchen and we can sit round the table together.

*

When I first make rice pudding, your visible joy at the large, bronzed dish scented with orange zest and cinnamon feels miraculous. Even more so when you have a second bowl. I think of the pudding as a way that I have met your needs. I have made a place where you feel good. It is difficult to admit that by making the pudding I am also meeting my own needs, that I am also making myself feel good. I feel a tightening in my chest and a wish to flee at the approach of intimacy and closeness, and also its opposite: an ardent desire to cook for you. Intimacy is difficult. I do not want to be known, to be seen – and also, I do.

*

Cooking for *You* is 'bittersweet', full of paradox. (Anne Carson) Perhaps the concept of paradox was first developed when eating, trying to name the experience of sweetness and

149

bitterness on the tongue at the same instant. Coaxing and repellent, proximity and distance, advance and retreat. The play of opposites, or others. An invitation and its refusal. Anne Carson discusses Sappho's use of 'bittersweet' (actually 'sweet-bitter' in Greek) to characterize the 'eros' of relationships between people:

> ... lover, beloved and that which comes between them. They are three points of transformation on a circuit of possible relationship, electrified by desire so they touch not touching ... The third component plays a paradoxical role for it both connects and separates, marking two that are not one
>
> (Carson, *Eros the Bittersweet*)

For Carson, language is the third thing that 'both connects and separates' people who do not move closer themselves but allow desire to dance forward through their words. Food is between me and You – the third thing that marks 'two that are not one'. But food is riskier than language as a plaything; it *spatters* from the pan onto your skin or my skin and it tends to disappear, bringing the feared-desired touch within reach, sometimes inevitably. Think of spaghetti and meatballs in the Disney film *The Lady and the Tramp* (1955). The strand of spaghetti that connects them also marks the distance between them, but it diminishes as they eat, eventually bringing a moment of touch. Though the nature of appetite ensures food does not disappear entirely. There is another meal to plan: another *You*, another me.

And it is only suddenly, at the moment when I would dissolve that boundary, I realize I never can. (Carson)

Conflicting impulses for proximity and flight lead me to embrace cooking for each new *You* I meet. I do not send myself. I make an avatar out of food. The dishes I cook for you are the eidolon, the εἴδωλον, the phantom that I send in my place so that I may remain far away. In some tellings of the Trojan wars, Helen – 'the face that launched a thousand ships' – does not go to Troy, but sends a phantom, an eidolon in her place: 'Helena who is not / where she is'. (Barbara Köhler, trans. mine) I send a steamy apparition of orange and cinnamon and caramelizing milk solids thickened with rice starch. I find myself unappetizing, so I make something delicious and offer it in my stead.

*

The recipe is my ship, my means for approaching *You* who are not-me. It is my ship, though it is not for conquering. Your refusals and your pleasures rebuild the recipe again and again. It is your ship too. The recipe is a collective text, a chorus. When I try to write at the kitchen table, the 'I' becomes blurred, so I see double, triple, I, I, I, I, we.

*

I clean the space, I make it ready. You are coming and I will make rice pudding.

151

The pleasure of performance and spectacle, of working to give you pleasure in the kitchen. I like to dress up I like the music to be right is it Chaka Khan, is it Depeche Mode, is it Giorgio Moroder, is it David Bowie, is it Kelela, is it Missy Elliott, is it Mingus.

I need to rest and then I am going to walk to the shop to buy milk for rice pudding.

I begin to walk to the shop to buy the milk, but it starts to rain and I feel tired. So I drive and on the way back stop at the allotment and pick artichokes and rhubarb and chard and rocket and coriander and chives for breakfast.

Washing up before cooking because I have not done it in days because I was tired. Resting before beginning. Resting in the middle. Washing up bottles of sour milk left on the doorstep in the hot sun because I forgot to cancel the milk when I was away. I came home to a pool of melted butter on the doorstep. On the sofa resting while Richard Strauss's 'Vier letzte Lieder: Im Abendrot' (*Four final songs: At Sunset*) is sung by Jessye Norman, oh my God, play it twice, slow deliberation in the trenches of feeling.

'Im Abendrot', the song of rice pudding.

When I first meet you, I make rice pudding for you in a yellow kitchen, for a family that is a different shape to what I know.

Wir sind durch Not und Freude
gegangen Hand in Hand

We have walked hand in hand
Through sorrow and joy

(Joseph von Eichendorff, trans. Mari Pračkauskas)

Turning to the page for 'Reiz Kugel' in Claudia Roden's *The Book of Jewish Food*. I want it to be sweet and rich and cold against the humidity of the weather. I must make it so it has time to cool. I am cooled by Jessye Norman's voice too.

I do not have pudding rice!

It has been a long time since I have cooked for you and a long time since I have run out of pudding rice. I built up a stockpile without intending to – I kept buying bags of pudding rice thinking I had none during the first pandemic lockdown. Obeying the pace of 'Im Abendrot' I make a cup of strong black tea with milk and eat three chocolate-covered chocolate-and-mint Girl Scout cookies sent by an American relation. The tea and the biscuits pick me up from a low spell. I decide not to panic or rush. I finish my tea and go to the shop again. I could not find 'pudding rice' as it is often referred to but a box of 'risotto rice', which is what Roden's recipe calls for in any case. It is now after 7 p.m., almost 7.30 p.m., so the pudding will not be cool. I read the recipe. I read it again.

153

I messaged you earlier to say I was making rice pudding, also to check if cow's milk is OK for you right now. To give you a moment to say no to milk, or no to pudding, but you say 'eek yum!' I weigh the rice and weigh the sugar and bring a large pan of water to the boil then add a teaspoon of salt and set a timer for five minutes. I am also making dinner, so I put a large chopping board on the table and take a small sharp knife and a bowl and fill it with water and the juice of half a lemon before dropping the lemon half in. I begin trimming artichokes. I cut the tough outer layer from the two inches of stalk that I left on, then cut the petals of the bud off halfway and peel the tough outer leaves from what is left and then drop them into the lemon water. After one or two artichokes, the five minutes is up.

After the five minutes of my rice cooking, I drain the rice into a colander as instructed. I am keen not to overcook it as I have done before. Some of the grains of rice are stuck to the pan so I scrape them off. I measure the milk and bring it to the boil, watching all the while, not daring to return to the artichokes as I know how easy it is to burn milk. A very fine froth appears on the surface of the milk as it becomes hotter and approaches boiling point. As I see the swirling uprising of milk at boiling point, I turn down the heat and add the rice and stir it. I set a timer for thirty minutes and look at the clock. You will arrive in thirty minutes; it will not be cool. I put on a pan of water to boil and return to the artichokes. I almost cut myself several times, but I do not actually do so. I am very focussed. When there are fifteen minutes left on the timer for the milk, I put the artichokes in the boiling water with some salt.

While the artichokes and the rice are cooking (I stir the rice now and again), I quickly trim and wash some rhubarb from the allotment and put it in another pan with a lid on and six spoons of sugar. It is a great quantity of rhubarb.

I put the heat on for the rhubarb. I add sugar to the rice and milk and stir for a few minutes then I turn off the heat for the rice pudding and drain the artichokes. There is a knock on the door. You are here, and you do not need an immediate snack. I make you a drink, Campari and tonic and ice, and return to the rice. I separate three eggs and mix in some of the cooling milky rice with the yolks, stirring well so they do not go hard. I add them to the big pan of rice and ask if you can stir it for me while I prepare the rest of the meal. I am so full of joy that you are here I hug you several times I feel very good in my body again, very happy. I ask if you remember the first time I made you rice pudding over ten years ago during the world cup in 2010 for all of your extended family and you say, 'Yes it was a revelation, did you cook it with orange, or?' and I say yes orange and cinnamon. And you say, 'After that we basically ate rice pudding all the time.' I say yes, it's so easy and cheap to make and I want to say generous, but I don't. I say, while you stir, that we want the yolks to turn the milk to a custard texture. You are excited by stirring. I have not made this type of rice pudding for you before, but you remember that I gave this recipe to other people for a project. You remember that one person served it with mango and another cooked the recipe with her child.

I sent Claudia Roden's rice pudding recipe to a few writers and asked them to cook it however they wanted and write about it. The exercise was an attempt to show how a recipe can hold many lives, many inhabitants, an attempt to show the capaciousness of the recipe and how I felt it had accommodated me. Each account of cooking the rice pudding retained an element of unmediated experience, or, to borrow writer and psychoanalyst Nuar Alsadir's phrase, 'a tracking of the grain, the body, emotions' – as the recipe text became movement before returning to language, weathered by their living. One cook wrote:

> I realize eating it how ragged we've all been feeling. I have seconds.
>
> C sits up with us and wants to feed himself, looking at his reflection in the back of the spoon as he does. Reiz kuggle. (Edwina Attlee)

I cut up the cooked artichokes into quarters and arrange them on a large plate. I make a dressing of red wine vinegar and olive oil and salt and pour it over. I ask if you are OK eating sourdough bread, and you say 'a bit' so I make toast and dress it with oil and salt. I make it under the grill because the toaster is being repaired. I get bored and only really toast one side. We eat and then as you finish the plate I get up and blanch some chard in salted water and drain it. I cut up a third of a red pepper very small and 3–4 small cloves of garlic. I put three large Italian sausages in a large frying pan with olive oil and turn them so they colour gently all over. I realize I have forgotten to prick them, so I stab them with the sharp end of a small knife, thinking of Mrs Beeton and D.W. Winnicott. Juice and melted fat seep out, basting the sausages beautifully. I decide to cook the dish as one and add the garlic and pepper pieces to the pan and stir, coating everything with oil. When it's fragrant I add two drained tins of cooked chickpeas and keep stirring until the sausages are cooked, then add in the chard and stir everything and season with salt. I put the pan on the table and we eat. I ask if you want more, and you say you would like half of the remaining sausage and I give you seconds of chickpeas and when seconds are finished you serve yourself more and finish the pan. Later I serve bowls of rice pudding and rhubarb. We have seconds. And then you have a bowl just of rhubarb.

[I write down the account of cooking the artichoke, sausage and rice pudding meal in my journal over two days. I have to take lots of breaks from writing to have small naps, even between paragraphs, because I am fatigued. In the afternoon I get up from writing about rice pudding on the sofa to cook lunch for myself – minestrone with beans, tomatoes, bacon, carrot, garlic, other things. Then I am very tired, and I lie down on the sofa and apply for a job. I eat fish and chips in the evening. The next day I write the rest while I am on the train to Birmingham. First, I take the train to London then travel on the underground to Euston

Square then walk to Euston station and board a train to Birmingham, where I alternate writing and sleeping. I buy a packet containing two slices of Soreen Malt Loaf with butter already on it. My mother used to make buttered malt loaf for my packed lunch at school.]

*

A little over ten years after I first make rice pudding, I am cooking for a new *You* and I ask, 'what do you eat?', and I find out: no oysters.

Watermelon and tomato salad
Cod with spicy sauce, green salad and potatoes.
Strawberries, cream and sugar

In fact, I ask if there are things that I should *not* cook, so I could not have known how you felt about cream. I give everyone around the table a bowl of strawberries and pass round a pot of cream. You pour in cream to the top of the bowl with a few strawberries and so at first, I wonder if it is a mistake and you hadn't been looking as you poured. But then I see that you are looking intently into the bowl and spooning cream into your mouth. You are quiet and it is as if no one else is there. Just you and the cream. A bowl of cream with a few strawberries. Cream soup. Drinking cream from the bowl. Then another bowl of cream on its own when the strawberries have gone. Then tears then dancing and laughing explosions of giggles and a rabbit impression of me, which takes me by surprise

158

you are looking back at me

The next day I buy more cream in case you need it. I am nervous of being with you who are still quite new to me, so I set a path, a river of cream, of tomato sauce, of watermelon, of mayonnaise, of fried potatoes so I can come closer.

I have a growing list of foods that people I know don't eat –

Hot pale toast
Cold toast
Tiny fish
Octopus
Aubergines
Mushrooms
Cauliflower
Goat's cheese
Onion
Wheat
Soft eggs
Hard eggs
Eggs
Honey
Fennel
Capers
Apricots
Anchovies
Pork
Gooseberries and other sharp fruits
Parsnips

I like this list; it gives me creative constraints to work within. A distinctive palate of scents, gestures, temperatures and temporalities. Your refusals help me think clearly and give me energy; like the changing seasons, your appetites limit the total possible edible world to a space in which I can play and then: you can play with your food.

In the height of summer I cook you aubergine parmigiana and a courgette, watercress and walnut salad so we can go out and dance.

I cook you pheasant and stuffing made from liver, brandy, shallot, bacon mixed with cornbread and fresh herbs so you can celebrate Thanksgiving even though you are far from home.

We are both ill, it is the middle of the week in November, and I make us sweet and sharp pot-roasted chicken with figs.

You have just started dating my friend and I make you eggs baked in sweet pepper tomato sauce with smoked paprika butter and yogurt.

For breakfast I make you chard baked with cream, a little diced tomato, eggs and butter and we eat it with Turkish simit sesame bread and coffee.

You are living in a flat with no oven just two electric rings and you look a bit low, so I roast some lamb shoulder in a frying pan on the stovetop and roast potatoes with rosemary in a saucepan with the lid tightly on, then leeks and cabbage with butter while the meat is resting and serve it with a potent green sauce.

You bring me a courgette cake and two bags of compost as a house-warming present, and I make you squid braised with fennel and aioli.

It is the peak of summer, you stop off at my house on your walk home from work and I make you a salad from tomatoes grown in the yard, tuna, green beans, chickpeas and egg and name it after you.

What I want for the people I cook for is for them to enjoy their own perversions at the table, to feel free to exhibit a lack of constraint. To follow their desire, their appetites. To drink cream from the bowl. I think of You who I have not seen in several years, picking meat from the bones of a chicken in Berlin when we knew each other well, relaxed as a cat taking its private delight. And I love to see women take the last of the salad, the last of the fried potatoes, the last sausage, the last lick of sauce from the plate. Take every scrap.

Again and again, there is a *You…* and you, specifically, who I cannot meet, but try to. In the trying I find a way to live, something to do. *You* have just left: artichokes, sausages, greens; and *You* are just coming: watermelon, cod, cream. What then? Without a *You*, I often disappear. I am not there to see, I think.

But on parting you say, 'I have come to see you', and I almost can't bear it. You say you would happily just eat chips and sit at the green table and talk and it goes round in my head for days. 'I came to see you, the food is lovely, but I came to see you': the thought makes me cry. It is like you have seen me and are offering me chips and saying, 'eat'.

*

I am alone in the house for the first time in months. Very tired today but I walk into town to buy eggs and look in the windows of various shops. I want to go to the new Caribbean food shop and ring the bell twice as instructed on a note stuck on the inside of the glass door but there is no answer. I want to buy salt cod to make fritters; I will try another time. I walk on and have a look at the menu stuck up in the window of Tasty Chinese Takeaway a few doors down. I notice that an area of the glass in the window is fragmented, held together by a clear plastic sheet. Thinking of images I have seen online, I wonder if the glass is broken due to anti-Asian violence incited by racist conspiracy theories spread during the pandemic. It is a large pane and I know from watching house renovation programs on TV that glazing is very expensive to replace. I think of a friend's project devoted to documenting Chinese take-away restaurants in the UK when I look at the attractive patterned tiles and the counter inside. A tired-looking man with tattooed arms and a shaven head leans out of the pet shop next door as I am looking at the window. He had looked out as I walked past, headphones in, listening to a detective mystery and eating a small packet of honey mustard pretzel pieces. I hoped he would not interact with me as I was also tired – and indeed he leant back into the shop doorway. But as I stand and take a photo of the takeaway menu he leans out again and says that he thinks it is quite good. I say, 'Oh really', and that I have not eaten there before, and make as if to go. He then says he has had their food once and it was good, but that he more usually goes to Peking House along the road, where he likes the chow mein noodles and salt and pepper ribs. I say, 'Oh I like ribs' and he says, 'Dry ribs, all I need is a big plate of ribs and I'm happy.' I make to go a second time, saying 'Well that sounds great I will have to order that' and he says, 'They haven't been open much recently.' He seems concerned. I say 'Maybe some of the people there have been ill', thinking of the pandemic. Then I move away and say, 'Cheers, bye', and think about ordering ribs soon. He recedes back into the pet shop.

I am not often alone eating, even when living with relative strangers I cook for them. Now I realize I need another appetite to know what to cook. Sometimes, as now, I feel lost without your appetite. It is different in a restaurant, I can style myself as a diner trying things that others have imagined; appreciative, excited, indulged. But at home I feel adrift. Since you went away on Saturday to care for people, I have been feeling absent from myself. I am unused to domestic solitude, which is distinct from public solitude: no need for getting dressed, no need to present an ego and hold things together, no need to perform for an audience in whose gaze one might come alive. No, I have barely dressed, on Monday not at all. Since you have been away I have eaten

one oven pizza – half hot one night
half cold the next morning
muesli
eggs on toast and tea x 2
   (could not be bothered to grind coffee beans)
oven chips and beans
cold rice pudding
boiled egg and toast, coffee
ham and cream cheese on toast with a little cucumber

I feel disinclined to cook, a taut anxiety balled up just below my ribs above my stomach and do not have the courage to venture out of myself. I have spent most of the past few days in bed or on the sofa wearing a large grey fleece which I have also slept in. I have sought to hide, hibernate, been in a daze, empty of the will to move, to act, to cook. I cannot face the artichoke in the fridge that I cut from the allotment. I cannot face a pan of boiling water. I have no desire to speak to or through ingredients. I browse Tasty Takeaway's entries in an online search, but there is frustratingly little information. I consider Peking House, the place the pet shop man told me about. They have also left very little trace online. When I phone the answering message says they are closed due to the pandemic. Perhaps I will order from the Turkish restaurant which I often depend on, or eat nothing at all, or a bowl of cereal, which I like when I have a particular appetite. Even the thought of eating something I have cooked in this moment is appalling. I don't want to eat anything I have cooked, under any circumstances.

Can I only appreciate cooking through an imagination of the other? It is hard when completely alone to contemplate feeding myself because it means locating my own desires in isolation and working to serve them – which is the thing I find most difficult, most alien. I have been dependent on living through the appetites and desires of others. Alone I am so often lost. Yesterday, no words written, and no getting dressed. Today, dressed for the latter half of the day and writing at the end of the day. Perhaps I need several days to get used to being alone.

Last night I sought out more beige food: a new Chinese takeaway – hot and sour soup (not enough sour or salt or hot but nice strands of egg); chicken chow mein (quite good, slightly under-seasoned but nicely smoky); salt and pepper chips (quite enjoyable and made with Lao Gan Ma chilli oil with crispy bits); sweet and sour pork (pork too tough, a decent tang on the sauce). Then two fortune cookies just for me; I write down the note inside one which says,

'nothing seek, nothing find'.

I watch some basic things on television, a house renovation show and a strange, animated film made for children about children trying to kill their cruel parents and then finding new ones. I go to bed early. I have breakfast quite late the next morning, around 9. It takes me a long time to get out of bed. I have yogurt and cooked rhubarb that I had made to eat with rice pudding a week before, and muesli, then two pieces of toast and coffee reheated from yesterday. My appetite is returning. I hang up some washing and lay about: I read an essay I am editing, make notes, phone the other editor, reply to emails, think about my book. Have a bath (I forgot to mention that earlier, after breakfast, I listen to a Paul Temple detective mystery: the reliability of detectives finding the answer is a deep comfort)

and I get dressed!

Have lunch, almost the same as yesterday: crackers and ham and cucumber. Then I feel despairing again. At some point I put on another wash on a timer and hang up some other washing. I watch a video of the writer Olivia Laing talking to Maggie Nelson on my phone about, among other things, loneliness, the things people do to mitigate their loneliness. Cooking for other people is how I mitigate my loneliness. I cook to be with other people, but to do it only for myself often feels impossible. It is a circular logic. What or who do I orbit?

I look up Jean Laplanche and read a little about his work – he is a psychoanalyst and winemaker who appears in Agnès

Varda's film *Les Glaneurs et la glaneuse* ('The Gleaners and I') that I have watched several times in the past year. In it, he either says, or is quoted as saying, that the self comes into being through the other. This thought instantly resonates with me when I first watch the film and does still. I think, *how correct for a winemaker-cum-psychoanalyst!* He must consider himself in relation to the grape, the vine, the pleasure of the drinker, the other and his patients. He orbits their needs. When I watch Varda's film I feel an affinity with his Copernican revolution, a decentring of the subject, I. A subject orbiting the edge of the life-giving Other, O sun O sun O moon, what should I cook for you? I wallow in stasis, in twilight without *You*. I hibernate as if living without sun.

Thinking of my fortune cookie's message, 'nothing seek, nothing find', I look for others to give me purpose: music, tea, a cafe, the sea, encounters with passers-by about ribs. Thinking again about the artichoke in the fridge that I have avoided cooking for myself since Saturday (it is Wednesday). Will the sugars in its flesh have fermented and soured through their days in the fridge since I picked them from the allotment, as peas do? If I cook them for myself today, will I prove correct in my feeling that cooking for myself is appalling? Will the artichoke be disgusting? I have left them so long it is likely they will begin to be disgusting. I have been living in beige for days. Colour without the sun is not possible. Alone I have no name, no appetite, no body.

Who is Odysseus without the other to animate him, anyway?

When I leave the house after several attempts, I sit on a bench on the pier and drink a cup of tea from the pier cafe. The sun faces me. An old woman who briefly sat on my bench for a rest after asking if it was OK, before walking to the end of the pier – walks back past and as she does so she says 'Catching the last rays of sun?' and then requiring no reply, says, 'It's lovely, isn't it.' And I think yes yes yes.

An antivaxxer from the allotment sticks a sticker on a public bench. Possibly in protest that it is cordoned off from use with striped tape. She tells me she has been blogging, after an earlier conversation on the allotment when I recommended that she start because she told me she wanted to write. She tells me she is on a platform that is carbon neutral.

The harbour master on the pier looks at me as he walks past and says, 'Are you swotting?' I say I am trying to write a book. He looks at the horizon, at the sun, then back at me and says, 'It's a good place to do that.'

*

On Wednesday I sit on the sofa and read a piece by Toril Moi about the French philosopher and political activist Simone Weil. Moi describes Weil's ardent desire to serve the other, the worker, through striving towards revolution, and also, Weil's persistent refusal to acknowledge her own need for food and care. Even when others make food available for her, she does not eat. She withers over time. Her parents save her life again and again, following her around, saving her from injuries brought on by repeatedly attempting forms of labour that she is physically incapable of doing. In Weil's book *The Need for Roots*, food and feeding are the 'chief metaphors Weil uses to describe what it means to respond to a need'. (Moi) Weil writes,

> The food which a collectivity supplies for the souls of those who form part of it has no equivalent in the entire universe. (Weil, trans. Arthur Wills)

Collectivity does feed the soul; I have felt it sitting round the table and talking with friends in a crisis, and I have felt it sharing hot tea on the picket line while on strike at a university where I was a researcher on a precarious contract, and I have felt it on an allotment site being given armfuls of vegetables by my neighbours when my plot was rough. But it is both appropriate and sadly ironic that food is Weil's preferred metaphor for responding to a need. In committing food to such grand metaphorical purpose, she both acknowledges its importance and avoids confronting its materiality and textures, its relation to the body, to her own body and its needs. She channels her energy towards feeding others and does not feed herself. I feel a glimmer of recognition as I read Moi describe Weil's difficulty with acknowledging her own non-transcendent, earthly position, her own vulnerability. Rilke's Torso also says to the poet: 'Where are *you*? You cannot know me without enquiring into yourself.' Is it possible to serve the other's needs if we cannot serve our own? Weil's absolute refusal to acknowledge her own position – that is, her own body – ultimately absents her from the collective. She conceals illness from those who could help her recover. Alienation from oneself becomes alienation from the other and from the possibility of collective life. Both self and other become constrained in an object position: distant, Odyssean, in opposition.

One of the things I find most challenging is cooking for myself, because it means witnessing my own needs and desires and serving them. Often, I cannot detect them at all through the fortifications I have built that conceal them from view. I become Nobody, with no body. It can feel excruciating to look at myself in the mirror or anything approximating one, such as a dish that I cook just for me. There are flashes when I become visible to myself; I think about something I cooked when I had received some bad news and was alone a few years ago:

BAD NEWS POTATOES
For one, obviously

After receiving the bad news and crying for a while and possibly talking to someone supportive on the phone (that's a good idea), think about food. You initially assume you can't eat because there's no food in the house and you'll sit on the sofa forever and starve. You can't imagine what you will eat. Then you remember that in the cupboard are a few potatoes that have grown eyes and are starting to try to produce more potatoes. They are perfect for your purpose. Rub off the eyes with your thumbs and if they aren't covered in mud, cut the potatoes into smallish cubes without peeling (the greater your need to eat, the smaller the cubes should be). If they are covered in mud wash them first, or maybe consider eating something else, perhaps from the freezer, as submerging your hands in cold water and scrubbing might become too much to deal with in your current state.

Place the cubed potatoes in a snug pan (saucepan or frying pan, it doesn't matter) with a tablespoon of olive oil and a centimetre of butter cut from a block and a good pinch of salt. Bring the potatoes to frying point and then turn the heat down and place a lid on top. The pan I was using didn't have its own lid so I found a similar-sized lid to put on top. Really anything will do, the lid doesn't need to fit perfectly. Check and turn the potatoes in the pan every 5–10 minutes, they might stick a little and all the better, scrape off the crisp bits with a spatula. If you have a taste for it, make a cup of strong tea while they are cooking; I had Yorkshire tea with milk. When the potatoes are soft inside and a little crispy, take the lid off and allow them to continue frying while you crush a clove of garlic with salt, or if you don't have that, chop up a few spring onion greens. Mix the crushed garlic or onion greens with the potatoes and continue to fry for a minute or two on a low heat until the garlic is aromatic. Stir in a few teaspoons of chilli sauce of your choice. Place potatoes in a bowl, top with grated cheese of any kind and if you wish, a spoon of mayonnaise.

Return to the sofa and eat them, covered with a blanket.

The 'You' in this passage is me; I am writing to myself. When I cooked, ate, and then wrote down this recipe, I felt like I had cared for myself. I wrote my panic and stress into the recipe to document these things and make them visible (to me). I recorded the evidence of my own vulnerability; it was an attempt to write a recipe that met my needs.

A position of vulnerability can be found that serves the self and the other; as Katherine Angel writes in *Tomorrow Sex Will Be Good Again* –

> The denial of vulnerability, and the disidentification with the feminine, go hand-in-hand with a fantasy of sovereignty. But we are all dependent on others – on those who give birth to us and those who care for us; those who sustain us, feed us, enable our growth, our survival, our work, and our flourishing. Total independence is a fiction... vulnerability can be a form of care.

I think of the phrase *Eat While You Feed?*, the title of a film by the artist and curator Raju Rage that I saw at an exhibition they had curated called *Recipes for Resistance* at Ort Gallery in Birmingham. The film is 'an autoethnographic documentary of the Shah family in Cambridge UK that explores health and wellbeing, care, time, labour, lineage, tradition and archetypes, gender and cross generational and cultural exchange and unconventional family recipes'. One woman in the Shah family talks about her cooking and her life while preparing a meal with other family members in the room, making tea and rotis and chips and chutney and gatyas (and more). But not everything is given to the viewer. Complete recipes are not given in the recorded conversations and recipes are not fully demonstrated in the video. There are cuts and silences in the audio. Complete images of the women are withheld, only partial shots of hands, or the back of a head. Rage's film does not allow images of the women or their culinary knowledge to be appropriated and taken away by the viewer.

The Shah cook whose life is at the centre of the film says she spends 'fifteen to twenty minutes in the bath each morning massaging my hands'. She describes an upbringing where women were expected to 'sacrifice their lives for looking after their in-laws'. Now, she does not give all of herself to others: 'Half the time I'm by the riverside, talking, chatting, playing Antakshari, going for walks, going to restaurants for meals.' Sometimes she does not cook; she has fun, she plays and is fed by other people. Rage's film makes me realize that to 'eat while you feed' is to acknowledge that you have an appetite and are vulnerable, while also serving the appetites of others. To put your body into the frame, and to occupy your position within the collective. To say 'I', and 'You', in the same breath. To look out towards the other, and also, towards yourself. To make the collective, and also, to make yourself. And sometimes, to allow others to see your hunger and to let them feed you.

Let's get chips and sit at the green table.

Every Day a New Dawn,
a New Dish

Every day's everyday labour begins with the rising of the sun. There is nothing more repetitive than the dawn, and in the *Odyssey*, dawn is a woman and bringing the day is her work. In her translation, Emily Wilson marks the difference that is produced by each repetition by writing each arrival of dawn differently, saying of her decision,

> People ask what I do with Dawn. I love her and I want her metaphors to feel alive every time. So I mix it up on each riff:
> 'Soon Dawn was born, her fingers bright with roses'.
> 'When rosy-fingered Dawn came bright and early'.
> 'When newborn Dawn appeared with rosy fingers'.
>
> (Emily Wilson on Twitter in 2018, citing her own translation of Dawn in the Odyssey)

Repetition is also the insistence to make the day again, to make the day so you can 'feel alive' again. Make the day again differently because love requires making, the work to make the day again, differently. The hot red sauce has spattered my skin a thousand times or more and taught me how to 'feel alive' and feel alive again differently each time. The recipe has been the ship by which I have sailed to *You*, it has been the sea in which all of my living has accumulated. Sometimes I float on its surface, carried by all that has come before, feeling its warmth.

I have spent ten or more years tying and untying my apron strings and I will spend ten or more years again tying and untying them. As I have cooked the recipe I learnt how to make and unmake my body, finding its edges, contours and surfaces and making new ones.

The cooks are holding hands, we are dancing in a circle singing the siren-song THE VOICE OF THE APRON IS OURS, sweats and works and thinks and wants, has a body.

And I have met *You*, 'which is every beloved, which constitutes itself across difference and species and the whole of life. *You* is eros and caritas all mixed up in a word. It is also the stranger who any of us might be.' (Boyer) *You* are the stranger at my door at my table who I will cook for and the stranger whose refusals and pleasures will teach me how to eat and how to cook again, how to love again, seek again, see again and rewrite the recipe a thousand times and then sometimes, not to cook at all.

175

The hot red epic takes place at the scale of a hand, a spoon, a nose, a tongue. The recipe is an archive of all life that is too hot too red too wet to become a monument; it is an uncanonizable, uncanonizing sea of sauce. But still, I have documented it here, up until this point at least. I have tried to make the recipe visible as epic. I have written down what I have been doing in the kitchen because it is what I have been doing.

The recipe is an epic without a hero. It is an epic that spreads like sauce. Each instance of its cooking harnesses different needs and desires. Repetition and dissemination enrich rather than impoverish the recipe and give many hands powers of transformation. The recipe text can exemplify the revolutionary potency of language that is on the brink of translation into life.

Not a nothing at the end of writing, but a dish: life returned to language a thousand times over.

And how will life continue? Like this, like this, here and there and then and now. Rolled-up sleeves.

*

At the end of the epic, I am on the sofa.

Last night I was here too, watching the Olympic gymnastics highlights when I received a photo of you. In the picture you are standing with the saucepan in which you have just cooked tomato sauce. You are smiling and looking at the camera, and behind you, bowls are madly erupting with tangled nests of red-orange-tinted spaghetti. Your partner tells me you are exhausted and stressed after a 'veeeery long day'. When I look at you smiling in the photo, ten or more years of emotion suddenly rise up like a tidal surge and I break into tears again and again, shaking as hot salty water streams down my face and I am engulfed by all that has gathered into the hot red sauce.

Now it is 11.27 a.m. and I am in the corner of the sofa again thinking about lunch, or how to finish an epic which can have no end. It is not the end of the day, only late morning. But in late morning I can think about lunch, so the epic will end with a hot red lunch hour.

*

It is unexpectedly grey for the time of year; no sun is visible. I drive past a building site for a new wind-farm servicing station on my way to the supermarket. I live next to the sea and on the horizon on a clear day is not end-less sea, but the turning arms of wind turbines gathering energy. At night when it is dark all that can be seen of them is a line of red twinkling lights affixed to each one to warn off passing ships. A horizon of red spattering at night.

In the supermarket people are still wearing masks to protect each other from transmitting the virus and I am wearing one too, but the air is filled with the excitement of anticipation. It's Friday and people are shopping for the weekend, for the possibility of sun. As I walk round: the red sugary scent of strawberries. Then I squeeze round an old man's shopping trolley to take a 'living' basil plant. As soon as I pick it up its leaves make a cloud of green aniseed fragrance. I collect garlic, spaghetti, a tin of tomatoes, salt and a box of novel 'Neapolitan ice cream sandwiches', which I have not noticed on the shelf before. I think of my Neapolitan friend and what he would think of the supermarket own-brand ice cream: pale pink, white and brown ice creams layered and sandwiched in wafer and dipped in chocolate; I think he would love it. On the way home wind whips rain onto the windshield. I look out across the water, but visibility is bad, and the ships and cranes are shrouded in mist.

I tie my apron tightly over my clothes – a tight black racer-back vest and baggy dark blue trousers; grey Adidas trainers with silver stripes and grey socks. I sit down at the green table with a chopping board in front of me. I open Marcella Hazan's *The Classic Italian Cook Book* and follow her first instruction. I pick all of the leaves from the basil plant. As I do so, I notice another quality to its fragrance, a deeper, heady musk underneath the brighter greens. I wash the leaves under the cold tap and shake them dry in a tea towel. Then I deviate and open *Essential Classics of Italian Cooking* – I do not want to finely chop the basil with a knife as instructed in *The Classic Italian Cook Book*. I follow Hazan's more recent instruction to tear the basil into smaller pieces. I cut up the garlic finely, the more I cut the more its addictive smell radiates from the board, and I inhale all I can. I add the tin of tomatoes, the garlic, 5.5 tablespoons of olive oil (a quantity that is midpoint between each book), salt and black pepper that I crush on a chopping board as the grinder has broken. I cut up the tomatoes in the pan with scissors and set it on a medium heat.

You tell me that a visitor is arriving unexpectedly soon, and I decide to wait to eat until they arrive so we can eat together; I will add the basil just before serving.

Outside the wind is roaring the turbines are turning and in the kitchen the air is singing the air is singing *Marcella*, it is singing garlic tomato turning sweet and intensifying, the oil is becoming redder and redder, and it is breaking free and spattering the sides of the pan; the fragrance in the air has become a siren-song, the edges between things have blurred and become indistinct, there are not singers, there is a chorus

Works referenced in order of their first appearance

Sophie Collins, *Who Is Mary Sue?* (London: Faber & Faber, 2018)

Johann Wolfgang von Goethe, *Faust*, trans. Anna Swanwick (London: G. Bell and Sons, 1879)

Judith Butler, *Gender Trouble* (New York: Routledge, 1990)

Patricia Klindienst Joplin, 'The Voice of the Shuttle is Ours', in *Rape and Representation*, ed. Lynn A. Higgins and Brenda A. Silver (New York: Columbia University Press, 1991)

Gertrude Stein, 'Sacred Emily', in *Geography and Plays* (Boston Mass.: The Four Seas Company, 1922)

Gertrude Stein, 'Portraits and Repetition', in *Living in America* (New York: Random House, 1935)

Martha Rosler, *Semiotics of the Kitchen*, 1975

Silvia Federici, *Wages Against Housework* (Bristol: Power of Women Collective and Falling Wall Press, 1975)

Sylvia Plath, 'Mushrooms', in *The Colossus and Other Poems* (New York: Knopf, 1962)

Psycho, dir. Alfred Hitchcock (1960)

M.F.K. Fisher, *The Gastronomical Me* (1943) (London: Daunt Books, 2017)

Sara Ahmed, *The Promise of Happiness* (Durham, NC: Duke University Press, 2010)

Harriet Lerner, as heard on 'The Cut on Tuesdays' podcast, Gimlet Media, 8 October 2019

Nigella Lawson, *How to Be a Domestic Goddess* (London: Chatto & Windus, 2000)

Nigella Lawson, *Cook, Eat, Repeat* (London: Chatto & Windus, 2020)

Nigella Lawson, *Cook, Eat, Repeat*, Episode 4, BBC Two, 30 November 2020

Christina Sharpe, 'Beauty is a Method', *e-flux journal*, issue 105 (2019). https://www.e-flux.com/journal/105/303916/beauty-is-a-method/

Audre Lorde, *Zami: A New Spelling of My Name* (London: Penguin, 2018)

Saidiya Hartman, *Wayward Lives, Beautiful Experiments* (London: Serpent's Tail, 2019)

Audre Lorde, 'Poetry is Not a Luxury' (1985), in *Your Silence Will Not Protect You* (London: Silver Press, 2017)

Sigmund Freud, 'Lecture 33: Femininity' (1933), in *New Introductory Lectures on Psychoanalysis*, trans. and ed. James Strachey (London: Hogarth Press, 1974)

Adriana Cavarero, *In Spite of Plato: Feminist Rewriting of Ancient Philosophy* trans. Serena Anderlini-D'Onofrio and Áine O'Healy (Cambridge: Polity Press, 1995).

Ingeborg Bachmann, Malina, trans. Philip Boehm (London: Penguin, 2019)

Natalia Ginzburg, *The Little Virtues*, trans. Dick Davis (London: Daunt Books, 2018)

D.W. Winnicott, *The Child, the Family, and the Outside World* (_____: Penguin, 1973)

Harold McGee, *On Food and Cooking: The Science and Lore of the Kitchen* (New York: Scribner, 2004)

What Not to Wear, BBC Two, shown between 2001 and 2005

Anne Boyer, 'there will be singing', in her newsletter *M I R A B I L A R Y*, received 24 September 2020. https://anneboyer.substack.com/

M.F.K. Fisher, *How to Cook a Wolf* (New York: North Point Press, 1988)

'Murder by the Book', *Colombo*, dir. Stephen Spielberg, first aired 15 September 1971

Barbara Köhler, *Niemands Frau* (Frankfurt am Main: Suhrkamp, 2007); p. 151 my translation

"logocentrism, n." *OED Online*, Oxford University Press, June 2022, www.oed.com/view/Entry/243619. Accessed 15 June 2022

Theodor W. Adorno and Max Horkheimer, *Dialectic of Enlightenment* (1944), ed. Gunzelin Schmid Noerr, trans. Edmund Jephcott (Stanford: Stanford University Press, 2002)

Gilles Deleuze, *Cinema I*, trans. Hugh Tomlinson and Barbara Habberham (London: Continuum, 1992)

Suzan-Lori Parks, *Father Comes Home from the Wars* (London: Nick Hearn Books, 2016)

Charles Isherwood, 'Ulysses as an American Slave', *New York Times*, 28 October 2014. https://www.nytimes.com/2014/10/29/theater/father-comes-home-from-the-wars-by-suzan-lori-parks-at-the-public-theater.html

Ruth Rogers, 'Best Pasta', in 'Top foodies choose their favourite recipes of all time', *Observer*, 29 January 2006. https://www.theguardian.com/lifeandstyle/2006/jan/29/foodanddrink.features3

Marcella Hazan, *Marcella Cucina* (London: Macmillan, 1999)

Marcella Hazan, *Essential Classics of Italian Cooking* (London: Macmillan, 2012)

Marcella Hazan, *The Classic Italian Cookbook: The Art of Italian Cooking and The Italian Art of Eating* (London: Macmillan, 1980)

Marcella Hazan, *The Second Classic Italian Cookbook* (London: Macmillan, 1983)

Rose Gray and Ruth Rogers, *The River Cafe Cookbook* (London: Ebury, 1996)

Kate Briggs, 'Translation and a Lipogram: or, on Forms of Again-Writing and No- (or Not That-) Writing', *Bricks from the Kiln*, 4 (December 2020)

Mary Taylor Simeti, *Sicilian Food: Recipes from Italy's Abundant Isle* (London: Grub Street, 2009)

T.S. Eliot, *The Waste Land* (New York: Boni & Liveright, 1922)

Oliver Goldsmith, *The Vicar of Wakefield* (Oxford: Oxford University Press, 2008)

Homer, *Odyssey*, trans. Emily Wilson (New York: Norton, 2017)

Emily Wilson, Twitter TO COME

Sophie Collins, 'Joy & Happiness, Fidelity & Intimacy in Translation', *Bricks from the Kiln*, 4 (December 2020)

Sam Sifton, *The New York Times Cooking: No-Recipe Recipes* (New York: Random House, 2021)

Roland Barthes, *S/Z: An Essay*, trans. Richard Miller (New York: Hill and Wang, 1974)

D.W. Winnicott, *Playing and Reality* (London: Routledge, 2005)

Fred Moten, *In the Break: The Aesthetics of the Black Radical Tradition* (Minneapolis: University of Minnesota Press, 2003)

Battleship Potemkin, dir. Sergei Eisenstein, 1925

Herman Melville, 'Bartleby the Scrivener', in *I Would Prefer Not To: Essential Stories* (London: Pushkin Press, 2021)

Roland Barthes, *The Pleasure of the Text*, trans. Richard Miller (New York: Hill and Wang, 1975)

D.W. Winnicott, 'Living Creatively' (1970), in *Home is Where We Start From: Essays by a Psychoanalyst*, ed. Clare Winnicott, Ray Shepherd, Madeleine Davis (New York: Norton, 1990)

Isabella Beeton, *Mrs Beeton's Book of Household Management* (London: S.O. Beeton, 1861)

Jacqueline Rose, 'Mothers', *London Review of Books*, 36 (12), 19 June 2014. https://www.lrb.co.uk/the-paper/v36/n12/jacqueline-rose/mothers

John Donne, *No Man is an Island: A Selection from the Prose of John Donne* (London: Folio Society, 1997)

Katherine Angel, *Unmastered* (London: Allen Lane, 2012)

Maggie Nelson, *The Argonauts* (London: Melville House, 2016)

Rainer Maria Rilke, 'Archaic Torso of Apollo', in *The Poetry of Rilke*, trans. Edward Snow (New York: North Point Press, 2011)

Roland Barthes, *A Lover's Discourse: Fragments*, trans. Richard Howard (New York: Hill and Wang, 1978)

Anne Carson, *Eros the Bittersweet* (Princeton: Princeton University Press, 1986)

The Lady and the Tramp, dir. Clyde Geronimi, Wilfred Jackson and Hamilton Luske (1955)

Strauss, Jessye Norman and the Gewandhausorchester Leipzig, conducted by Kurt Masur, *Vier Letzte Lieder: Four Last Songs* (Philips, 1983)

Strauss, Joseph von Eichendorff, 'Im Abendrot / At Sunset', trans. Mari Pračkauskas, in the sleeve notes of *Vier Letzte Lieder* (Philips, 1983)

Claudia Roden, *The Book of Jewish Food* (London: Penguin, 1999)

Nuar Alsadir, 'The map of four kisses', *The Poetry Review*, 109(2) (Summer 2019). https://poetrysociety.org.uk/essay-the-map-of-four-kisses/

Edwina Attlee, writing in TENANCY PART 5: ON RECIPES II, ed. Rebecca May Johnson, August 2020, as part of the series TENANCY, ed. Helen Charman for *MAP magazine*. https://mapmagazine.co.uk/tenancy-recipes-part-ii

'Olivia Laing talking to Maggie Nelson', The Centre for Fiction podcast, 6 May 2021. https://www.youtube.com/watch?v=veQkCdXVqRw

Les Glaneurs et la glaneuse, dir. Agnès Varda (2000)

Toril Moi, 'I came with a sword', *London Review of Books*, 43 (13), 1 July 2021

Simone Weil, *The Need for Roots*, trans. Arthur Wills (London: Routledge, 2002)

Rebecca May Johnson, 'Bad New Potatoes', Dinner Document. https://dinnerdocument.com/2017/02/24/how-to-get-over-bad-news-potatoes/

Katherine Angel, *Tomorrow Sex Will Be Good Again* (London: Verso, 2021)

Raju Rage, *Eat While You Feed?* (2020), in *Recipes for Resistance*, curated by Raju Rage, Ort Gallery, Birmingham, 2021. https://ortgallery.co.uk/exhibitions/recipes-for-resistance/

OTHER REFERENCES

I was looking for a text through which to have a conversation about the use of recipes by theorists who do not directly engage with what a recipe is, when I saw Hannah Proctor tweet a screenshot of D.W. Winnicott's writing on sausages.

https://twitter.com/hhnncnnll/status/1369220258465280004
https://hannahproctor.com/

I first read Gertrude Stein on repetition and insistence in Zara Joan Miller's essay 'Repetition and Insistence in Akerman and Bausch' in *Another Gaze* 04.

https://anothergazejournal.bigcartel.com/product/another-gaze-04
https://zarajoanmiller.com/

I was grateful to be able to go and see the exhibition *Recipes for Resistance*, curated by artist Raju Rage at Ort Gallery in Birmingham towards the end of writing the book. *Recipes for Resistance* brought together the work of Sabba Khan, Jasleen Kaur, Navi Kaur, Yas Lime and Raju Rage, and explores 'the politics of food and its relationship to migration, belonging, memory, culture, coloniality, gender, resilience, adaptability and resistance'. Thanks to the exhibition, I came across artist Jasleen Kaur's book *Be Like Teflon* (Glasgow: Glasgow Women's Library, 2019), which carefully complicates the image of the cook through a collection of conversations with women of Indian heritage in the UK on themes of 'labour, duty, sustenance and loss' as well as giving recipes.

Acknowledgements

A book is a collective effort. I would like to thank –

everyone for and with whom I have cooked: you have been my teachers.

the Society of Authors Foundation for the work-in-progress grant which was invaluable to the writing of this book. Thanks to the British School at Rome for the John R. Murray creative writing residency, which gave me a much-needed change of scene for editing this book.

my beloved agent and friend Harriet Moore, who first suggested I write a book. Thank you for encouraging me to be bold (be bold be bold)! Your belief in my work changed my life. Rory Williamson – I could not have hoped for a better editor, working with you has been such a joy. Everyone at Pushkin Press, especially Laura Macaulay.

I am grateful to many people for giving me the opportunity to do work that – directly and indirectly – went into this book. Emily LaBarge and Jeremy Millar who organized the Writing/Performance conference at the Royal College of Art where I gave a paper that became the basis of the Hot Red Epic chapter. Judith Beniston for our conversations during my PhD, in which I did thinking about translation, the *Odyssey*, quantum physics (and many other paths set by Barbara Köhler). Jen Calleja for commissioning me in 2015 to translate a short story into a recipe, and much besides. Cherry Styles for publishing my writing in several issues of *Grub Zine*. Lucy Dearlove for having me on her podcast *Lecker*. Sarah Shin and Rebecca Tamás for commissioning me to contribute a poem about tomato sauce to their book *Spells*. Helen Charman for commissioning me in 2020 to write about recipes as part of her residency as editor of the TENANCY project for *MAP magazine*. Thanks to the writers who cooked rice pudding and wrote about it: Edwina Attlee, Jen Calleja, Huw Lemmey, Nina Mingya Powles and Rebecca Tamás. Jonathan Nunn for commissioning me to write about cooking, the internet and the erotics of culinary knowledge for his food-writing newsletter *Vittles*. Matthew Stuart and Andrew Walsh-Lister of *Bricks from the Kiln* for asking me to write about blueprints and recipes, which led me to write about cooking in Rome.

Italia Uno, and Domenico de Blasio for taking me there; thank you to Felice for always welcoming me in Italian. My Camberwell family 2005–2008+, especially Simon

Hacking, Laura Norris, Joe Mulleady and Claire Mulleady. Chris Douse, with whom I shared a kitchen when I started Dinner Document. Beloved sisters Ayça Rodop and Danielle Young Canepa. Mathura Umachandran, we'll always be twirling to *La Vie en rose* (Grace Jones version). Mike Amherst. Katia Wengraf for stopping off at mine for dinner so we could hang out. Katherine Angel, Amy Key. My friend Sophie Davidson for plotting and worrying with me. Rachael Allen for the image of editing as 'stuffing it full of cream'. Olivia Laing and Ian Patterson for a very good lunch that helped me begin the writing. Rachel Roddy for the best conversations at a hundred miles an hour. The Marx reading group, Ben Critchley and Rachel Adams, for the fun of thinking together. Iain Ross, especially for making *The Magic Disco* Italo mix in 2007 which helped me dance my way into editing in 2021. My comrades at the British School at Rome for bringing me back to life, especially Freya Dooley: for the walking and the gossip and the eating and dancing. The canteen, cleaning and residency staff at the British School at Rome. Laura Ager for sea swims and for running the Electric Palace online film club where I watched *Battleship Potemkin*. The local wholefood shop and supermarket staff who worked in dangerous conditions during the pandemic when I was writing this book. Phil Thomas, Matt Mahon, Harriet Boulding and Sam Wilson for your support and friendship. Edwina Attlee, for all of the poetry club meetings, for Sitting Room and for generally being an inspiring thinker. Lily Gorlin for being a wonderful friend through thick and thin. Catherine C, for conversations that were vital to writing the book. Zoë Jewell for all of the meals we have shared. My parents for all of the love and care and for what you have taught me: Mum, for your exquisite sense of balance when composing a meal, which I have had the good fortune to witness first-hand. Dad, for giving me the courage to go out to sea and hold my nerve in heavy weather. My brothers, and all of my family, for love and support. I am grateful to everyone who has read and cooked from Dinner Document and written to me about it over the past ten years and everyone who read my TinyLetter series – your messages kept me going. Sam Johnson-Schlee for all of the peanut butter noodles while I was writing, and for making me so happy.